BAPTISM AND FULLNESS

The work of the Holy Spirit today

Baptism and Fullness

The work of the Holy Spirit today

John R. W. Stott

*Rector Emeritus of All Souls Church,
Langham Place, London*

Inter-Varsity Press

INTER-VARSITY PRESS
Universities and Colleges Christian Fellowship
38 De Montfort Street, Leicester LE1 7GP

© INTER-VARSITY PRESS, LEICESTER, ENGLAND

First Edition July 1964
Reprinted 1966, 1970, 1971, 1972, 1973
Second Edition November 1975
Reprinted 1977

ISBN 0 85110 387 1

Printed in Great Britain by
Hazell Watson & Viney Ltd,
Aylesbury, Bucks

Contents

Preface to the Second Edition

It is now eleven years since Prebendary Peter Johnston invited me to address the Islington Conference on the work of the Holy Spirit, and my talk was afterwards expanded and published under the title *The Baptism and Fullness of the Holy Spirit*.

Since then the movement which is called by some 'neo-pentecostal', but by most 'charismatic', has continued to spread. It is now an almost world-wide phenomenon, with highly-respected churchmen among its leaders. One cannot evaluate the contemporary church scene without taking it into account.

There can be no question that God has used this movement to bring blessing to large numbers of people. Many Christians testify to having experienced a new liberty and love, an inward release from the bondage of inhibitions, an overflowing joy and peace in believing, a stronger sense of the reality of God, a warmth of Christian fellowship unknown before, and a fresh zeal for evangelism. The movement constitutes a healthy challenge to all mediocre Christian living and all stuffy church life.

At the same time careful assessments are being made from varying points of view. Charismatic leaders are often the first to admit that there have been some causes for disquiet and that the task of serious theological debate has only just begun. One of the difficulties in the continuing discussion is that the charismatic movement is not an organized church or society with official doctrinal formularies. The Pentecostal churches, which have come into being since the turn of the century, do have published confessions of faith to which their pastors must adhere. But the charismatic movement is still very fluid, and its leaders and members are not all in full theological accord with one another. Some, it seems, hold a full 'pentecostal' position, virtually indistinguishable from that of Pentecostal churches. Others claim to have had what they are happy to call a 'pentecostal' experience, but do not formulate it in terms of classical 'pentecostal theology'. Yet others are in a state of flux in their own understanding, and are still seeking the right way to express their experience theologically.

Such flexibility is very welcome, partly because it is a token of their openness, and partly because it should stop anyone neatly polarizing the situation into 'charismatics' and 'non-charismatics', since an increasing number of people appear to have a foot in both camps. Although welcome, this fluidity also makes the task of assessment more difficult, since it is not always clear to whom or about whom one is talking. I would like to apologize in advance if some self-confessed 'charismatic' Christians who read these pages do not recognize themselves in what I write! I can only plead that I have tried to be objective and honest, to use information culled from actual people and published literature, and not to draw any caricatures.

Let me now explain why I have re-written and expanded the booklet published in 1964. What are the reasons for a second edition?

First, on re-reading what I wrote eleven years ago some parts struck me as obscure and others as weak, while the whole seemed incomplete. So I have tried to clarify what was obscure and to strengthen what was weak. In particular,

I have divided the original material into two separate chapters which are now respectively entitled 'The promise of the Spirit' and 'The fullness of the Spirit'. I have also expanded it, emphasizing common ground and indicating areas of continuing disagreement. I have then added new material in two further chapters entitled 'The fruit of the Spirit' and 'The gifts of the Spirit'.

My second reason is more personal. During recent years I have regularly received letters from people who say they have heard that, since writing *The Baptism and Fullness of the Holy Spirit*, I have changed my views. This is not so. The revised edition gives me the chance to correct this false rumour.

Thirdly, there is the need for all of us, whatever our precise stance on this issue may be, to remain in fruitful fellowship and dialogue with one another. None of us finds this easy. It takes considerable maturity to make and to maintain cordial personal relationships with people with whom one does not see eye to eye. At a recent conference I felt it right to confess my own immaturity both in having been too negative towards the charismatic movement and in having been too reluctant to meet its leaders and talk with them. I went on to suggest three areas which I felt might well be an agreed basis for further discussion. It may be helpful if I mention these here.

The first is *the objectivity of truth*. We live in very subjective days in which existentialism distinguishes sharply between 'authentic' and 'unauthentic' living, and uses purely subjective criteria by which to assess what is 'authentic', namely whether it seems authentic to me at the moment. But Christians, especially evangelical Christians, are convinced that God has spoken historically and objectively, that his Word culminated in Christ and in the apostolic witness to Christ, and that Scripture is precisely God's Word written for our learning. All our traditions, all our opinions and all our experiences must therefore be submitted to the independent and objective test of biblical truth.

Secondly, *the centrality of Christ.* In theory at least, all of us agree also on this. Our eyes have been opened to see the truth as it is in Jesus and our lips to confess that he is Lord. We have no difficulty in subscribing to the great affirmations of the apostle Paul in his letter to the Colossians that Jesus Christ is head of the universe and of the church; that God's purpose is 'that in everything he might be pre-eminent' (1:11–18); that 'in him the whole fullness of deity dwells bodily' (2:9); and that we ourselves 'have come to fullness of life' in him (2:10).

It is not enough, however, to pay lip-service to these statements about the supremacy and sufficiency of Christ; all of us have to go further and work out their implications. Some Christians give the impression that they hold a kind of 'Jesus plus' doctrine, namely, 'You have come to Jesus, which is fine; but now you need something extra to complete your initiation.' Others lay such emphasis on the sufficiency of Christ that they seem to have a static concept of the Christian life which allows no room either for growth into maturity or for deeper, fuller experiences of Christ.

Thirdly, we should be able to agree on *the diversity of life.* That is to say, the living God of nature and of Scripture is a God of rich and colourful diversity. He has made every human being, every blade of grass, every snow-flake different. I confess, therefore, that the longer I live the more hostile I become to all stereotypes. Yet some of us seem very anxious to force each other through our particular hoops and cast each other in our particular moulds. Is this not always regrettable? My own belief, as I try to elaborate in the later pages of this book, is that there is a wide variety of spiritual experiences and a wide variety of spiritual gifts. If we will but renounce the desire to imprison each other in strait-jackets, we shall find a new freedom and a new fellowship in the God of abundant diversity.

Finally, I should like to emphasize that my purpose in this

book is not polemical, for I am a man of peace, not war. If sometimes I have been negative, it is only in order to clarify the corresponding positive truth. I have also posed some questions which seem to me to need to be asked and answered. But I have no desire to hurt or embarrass anybody. My main concern is to try to expound certain important passages of Scripture. And my objective in this is that all of us may grasp more clearly both the greatness of our inheritance in Christ in order to enter into it more fully, and also the greatness of our responsibility to manifest all the fruit of the Spirit in our lives and to exercise those gifts of the Spirit which in his gracious sovereignty he has bestowed upon us.

April 1975   J. R. W. S.

Introduction

Wherever one looks in the church today, there is an evident need for a deeper work of the Holy Spirit.

In the West the old concept of 'Christendom' which has lasted for centuries seems to be rapidly dying, as more and more people repudiate the faith of their fathers. In the sixties, attempting to reinterpret the gospel to the modern age, secular theologians openly denied the fundamentals of historic Christianity. Having largely lost the Christian faith, the western world has lost the Christian ethic also. Society is now confessedly pluralist and permissive. The institution of the church survives, but is regarded by most people as a relic from the past, an outmoded structure like the superstitions to which it clings. Meanwhile, there are some signs of spiritual renewal – pockets of fresh vigour in the older denominations, in the house church movement and in parachurch organizations. Yet the general picture remains one of steadily diminishing Christian influence in an increasingly secular community. The dead, dry bones of the church need the living breath of God.

In some other parts of the world, it is true, the church is growing rapidly. At the International Congress on World Evangelization in Lausanne in July 1974 we heard of 'an unprecedented receptivity to the Lord Jesus Christ'. Multi-

13

tudes are flocking into the church, and in some areas the Christian birth-rate is higher than the population birth-rate. All this gives great cause for rejoicing. At the same time, these people's movements are sometimes marred, as in the days of the early church, by rivalries and factions, by false teaching and by superficial emotionalism. So here, too, we see the need for a deeper work of the Holy Spirit, since he is the author of unity, truth and maturity.

It is not only, however, when we look at the older churches of the western world and the younger churches of the Third World that we see the need of the Holy Spirit. It is also when we look at ourselves. Surely all of us who say we belong to the Lord Jesus, whatever our particular persuasion may be, must be oppressed at times by our personal failures in Christian life and Christian ministry. We are conscious that we fall short of the standards of Christ, of the experience of the first Christians and of the plain promises of God in his Word. We are thankful indeed for what God has done and is doing, and we do not want to denigrate his grace by minimizing it. But we hunger and thirst for more. We also long for true revival, an altogether supernatural visitation of the Holy Spirit in the church, bringing depth as well as growth; and meanwhile we yearn for a deeper, richer, fuller experience of Christ through the Holy Spirit in our own lives.

Basic principles of approach

As we approach this study, let me make four introductory points.

First, our common desire and duty as Christians must be to enter into the full purpose of God for us. Nothing less than this will please him; so nothing less than this should please us. All of us who claim to follow Christ should seek a clearer understanding of God's purpose for his people, should be moved to penitence by our failures to attain it, and should keep pressing on eagerly, longing to lay hold firmly and fully of everything for which Christ has laid hold of us (see Phil. 3:12–14).

Secondly, we are to discover this purpose of God in Scripture. The will of God for the people is in the Word of God. It is here that we are to learn it, and not primarily from the experience of particular individuals or groups, however true and valid these experiences may be. We should neither covet for ourselves what God may have given to others, nor urge upon others what God may have given to us, unless it is plainly revealed in his Word that this is part of the inheritance promised to all his people. What we seek for ourselves and what we teach to others must be governed by the Scripture alone. Only when the Word of God dwells in us richly shall we be able to evaluate the experiences which we and others may have. Experience must never be the criterion of truth; truth must always be the criterion of experience.

Thirdly, this revelation of the purpose of God in Scripture should be sought primarily in its *didactic* rather than its *descriptive* parts. More precisely, we should look for it in the teaching of Jesus, and in the sermons and writings of the apostles, rather than in the purely narrative portions of the Acts. What is described in Scripture as having happened to others is not necessarily intended for us, whereas what is promised to us we are to appropriate, and what is commanded us we are to obey.

It would be easy to misunderstand the point I am trying to make. I am *not* saying that the descriptive passages of the Bible are valueless, for 'all Scripture is inspired by God and profitable' (2 Tim. 3:16). What I *am* saying is that what is descriptive is valuable only in so far as it is interpreted by what is didactic. Some of the biblical narratives which describe events are self-interpreting because they include an explanatory comment, whereas others cannot be interpreted in isolation but only by the light of doctrinal or ethical teaching which is given elsewhere.

Thus, Paul tells us that the things which Israel experienced in the wilderness 'happened to them as a warning' and 'were written down for our instruction' (1 Cor. 10:11; *cf.* Rom. 15:4). He is referring to several episodes in which God's judgment fell upon them. Here, then, are narrative passages which are profitable for teaching. Yet their value lies not simply in the description, but in the explanation. We are to avoid idolatry, immorality, presumption and grumbling, he says, for these things are grievously offensive to God. How do we know? Because God's judgment overtook them, as Moses clearly indicates in the stories, and as he and the prophets teach elsewhere. We must not, however, deduce from these stories that if we sin in these ways we too shall die by plague or snakebite as they did. Similarly, we can learn from the story of Ananias and Sapphira in Acts 5 that lying is very displeasing to God, for Peter says so; but we cannot assume that, like them, all liars will drop down dead.

Here is another example. In two separate paragraphs of the Acts Luke tells us that the early Christians in Jerusalem sold many of their possessions, held the rest in common, and distributed goods and money 'as any had need' (2:44, 45; 4:32–37). Are we to deduce from this that they set a pattern which all Christians are meant to copy, and that private property is forbidden to Christians? Some groups have thought so. Certainly the generosity and mutual care of those early Christians are to be followed, for the New Testament commands us many times to love and serve one another, and to be generous (even sacrificial) in our giving. But to argue from the practice of the early Jerusalem church that all private ownership is abolished among Christians not only cannot be maintained from Scripture but is plainly contradicted by the apostle Peter in the same context (Acts 5:4) and by the apostle Paul elsewhere (*e.g.* 1 Tim. 6:17). This example should put us on the alert. We must derive our standards of belief and behaviour from the teaching of the

New Testament, wherever it is given, rather than from the practices and experiences which it portrays.

Fourthly, our motive in thus seeking to learn God's purpose from the teaching of Scripture is practical and personal, not academic or controversial. We are brothers and sisters in the family of God. We love one another. We are concerned to know God's will in order to embrace it ourselves and commend it to others. We have no desire to score cheap points off one another in theological debate.

After these four simple introductory points regarding our approach we are ready to consider in turn, from Scripture and in relation to contemporary discussion, what is meant by the promise of the Spirit (and whether this is the same as the 'baptism' of the Spirit), the fullness of the Spirit, the fruit of the Spirit and the gifts of the Spirit.

1 The Promise of the Spirit

The Christian life is life in the Spirit. All Christians are happily agreed about this. It would be impossible to be a Christian, let alone to live and grow as a Christian, without the ministry of the gracious Spirit of God. All we have and are as Christians we owe to him.

So every Christian believer has an experience of the Holy Spirit from the very first moments of his Christian life. For the Christian life begins with a new birth, and the new birth is a birth 'of the Spirit' (Jn. 3:3–8). He is 'the Spirit of life', and it is he who imparts life to our dead souls. More than this, he comes himself to dwell within us, and the indwelling of the Spirit is the common possession of all God's children.

Is it that God makes us his sons and then gives us his Spirit, or that he gives us his 'Spirit of sonship' who makes us his sons? The answer is that Paul puts it both ways. On the one hand, 'because you are sons, God has sent the Spirit of his Son into our hearts' (Gal. 4:6). On the other, 'all who are led by the Spirit of God are sons of God. For you did not receive the spirit of slavery to fall back into fear, but you have received the spirit of sonship' (Rom. 8:14, 15). Whichever way you look at it, the result is the same. *All* who have the Spirit of God are the sons of God, and *all* who are sons of God have the Spirit of God. It is impossible, indeed inconceivable, to have the Spirit without being a son or to be a son without having the Spirit. Moreover, one of the first and graciously continuing works of the indwelling Spirit is to assure us of our sonship, notably when we pray. 'When we cry, "Abba! Father!" it is the Spirit himself bearing witness with our spirit that we are children of God' (Rom. 8:15, 16; *cf.* Gal. 4:6). He has also flooded our hearts with God's love (Rom. 5:5). Paul sums it up by affirming that 'any one who does not have the Spirit of Christ does not belong to him' (Rom. 8:9; *cf.* Jude 19).

This whole passage in Romans 8 is of considerable importance because it demonstrates that in Paul's mind to be 'in Christ' and 'in the Spirit', to have 'the Spirit in you' and 'Christ in you' are all synonymous expressions. No-one can have Christ, then, without having the Spirit. Jesus himself made this plain in his Upper Room discourse when he drew no distinction between the 'coming' to us of the three Persons of the Trinity. 'I will come', he said; 'we will come' (the Father and the Son); and 'the Comforter will . . . come' (Jn. 14:18-23; 16:7, 8).

Once he has come to us and taken up his residence within us, making our body his temple (1 Cor. 6:19, 20), his work of sanctification begins. In brief, his ministry is both to reveal Christ to us and to form Christ in us, so that we grow steadily in our knowledge of Christ and in our likeness to Christ (see, *e.g.*, Eph. 1:17; Gal. 4:19; 2 Cor. 3:18). It is by the power of the indwelling Spirit that the evil desires of our fallen nature are restrained and the good fruit of Christian character is produced (Gal. 5:16-25). Nor is he a kind of private possession, ministering only to the individual Christian; he also unites us to the body of Christ, the church, so that Christian fellowship is 'the fellowship of the Holy Spirit', and Christian worship is worship in or by the Holy Spirit (*e.g.* Phil. 2:1; 3:3). It is he, too, who reaches out through us to others, prompting us to witness to Christ and equipping us with gifts for the service to which he summons us. In addition, he is called 'the guarantee of our inheritance' (Eph. 1:13, 14), for his presence within us is both the pledge and the foretaste of heaven. And on the last day he will be active in raising our mortal bodies (Rom. 8:11).

This rapid rehearsal of some of his major activities in the experience of a Christian should be enough to show that, from the very beginning to the very end of our Christian life, we are dependent on the work of the Holy Spirit – the Spirit, Paul writes, 'which has been given to us' (Rom. 5:5). On this I believe and hope all Christians are agreed.

Is this promised 'gift' of the Spirit the same as the 'baptism' of the Holy Spirit, however? It is here that convictions differ. Some say 'yes', and others 'no'. Those who say 'no', who believe that the 'gift' and the 'baptism' are distinct, go on to teach that the 'baptism' is a second and subsequent experience even if, at least ideally, it follows very closely on the first. On the other hand, those who believe that the two are identical, and that to have been 'baptized' with the Spirit is a vivid figure of speech for to have 'received' the Spirit, regard this 'baptism' as something which all Christians have had. This is my own position, and I shall shortly elaborate what I understand to be its biblical basis.

This is not just a rather frivolous quibble over words, as it may appear on the surface to be. On the contrary, it is bound to have a considerable effect on our understanding of our own Christian pilgrimage as well as on our counselling of other people. So we must investigate some important passages of Scripture which bear on this question. But first we must set the scene for our discussion.

It is always important in biblical studies to interpret a text in its context, and the broader the context the more accurate our interpretation is likely to be. The broadest context of all is the whole Bible. We believe that the whole

Bible is God's Word written. Therefore, since God does not contradict himself, we further believe that the Bible is a harmonious divine revelation. We must never 'so expound one place of Scripture, that it be repugnant to another' (Article 20 of the Church of England's 39 Articles), but rather interpret each Scripture in the light of all Scripture.

If we apply this principle to our enquiry as to what the 'baptism of the Spirit' is, the first point we shall notice is that this is an exclusively New Testament expression (occurring seven times), but that it is also a fulfilment of Old Testament expectation. This expectation was usually expressed in terms of God's promise to 'pour out' his Spirit, and the apostle Peter in his sermon on the Day of Pentecost specifically equated the 'outpouring' of the Spirit (promised by Joel) with the 'baptism' of the Spirit (promised by John the Baptist and Jesus.) The two expressions were alluding to the same event and the same experience.[1]

The promise of a distinctive blessing

We can go further. This 'outpouring' or 'baptism' of the Holy Spirit was to be one of the main distinctive blessings of the new age. So much so that the apostle Paul could describe the new age inaugurated by Jesus as 'the dispensation of the Spirit' (2 Cor. 3:8).

This is not, of course, to say that the Holy Spirit did not exist before. The Holy Spirit is God and therefore eternal. Nor is it to say that he was not active before. In Old Testament days he was ceaselessly active – in the creation and preservation of the universe, in providence and revelation, in the regeneration of believers, and in the equipment of special people for special tasks.

Nevertheless, some of the prophets foretold that in the days of the Messiah God would grant a liberal effusion of the Holy Spirit, which would be new and distinctive, and also (as we shall see) available for all. Thus, Isaiah spoke

[1] *Cf.* Acts 1:4, 5; 2:17, 33.

of the day when the Spirit would be 'poured upon us from on high' (32:15). In Isaiah 44:3 God promised: 'I will pour water on the thirsty land, and streams on the dry ground; I will pour my Spirit upon your descendants, and my blessing on your offspring.' The same phraseology was used by Ezekiel to whom God said: 'Then they shall know that I am the Lord their God ... when I pour out my Spirit upon the house of Israel ...' (39:28, 29). Again, in a better known passage, God said: 'and it shall come to pass ..., that I will pour out my spirit on all flesh' (Joel 2:28).

John the Baptist, the last prophet of the old order, summarized this expectation in his familiar saying which ascribed the outpouring of the Spirit to the Messiah himself: 'I have baptized you with water; but he will baptize you with the Holy Spirit' (Mk. 1:8).

Now it is instructive to note that this prophecy of John, recorded by the three synoptic evangelists as a simple future ('he will baptize'), takes the form in the fourth Gospel of a present participle: 'I myself did not know him; but he who sent me to baptize with water said to me, "He on whom you see the Spirit descend and remain, this is he who baptizes with the Holy Spirit" ' (Jn. 1:33). This use of the present participle is timeless. It describes not the single event of Pentecost, but the distinctive ministry of Jesus: 'this is he who baptizes with the Holy Spirit.'[2] Indeed, the very same words *ho baptizōn*, which refer here to Jesus, are used by Mark to denote John the Baptist himself! Usually John is called *ho baptistēs*, 'the Baptist', but three times in the narrative of Mark (1:4; 6:14, 24) he is called *ho baptizōn*, an expression rendered in RSV, 'the baptizer'. In other words, just as John is called 'the Baptist' or 'the baptizer', because it was characteristic of his ministry to baptize with water,

---

[2] Another example of this Greek construction is in Gal. 1:23, where Saul of Tarsus is described as *ho diōkōn hēmas pote*, 'he who once persecuted us', or simply 'our former persecutor', indicating what was characteristic of him in his pre-conversion days.

so Jesus is called 'the Baptist' or 'the baptizer', because it is characteristic of his ministry to baptize with the Holy Spirit.

This reference to the distinctive and continuing ministry of Jesus is strengthened by verse 29 of the same chapter (Jn. 1), in which the Baptist says, 'Behold, the Lamb of God, who takes away the sin of the world!' It is another present participle, *ho airōn*. If we put verses 29 and 33 together, we discover that the characteristic work of Jesus is twofold. It involves a removal and a bestowal, a taking away of sin and a baptizing with the Holy Spirit. These are the two great gifts of Jesus Christ our Saviour. They are brought together by the prophets in the Old Testament and the apostles in the New, and they cannot be separated. Thus, through the prophet Ezekiel God promised: 'I will sprinkle clean water upon you, and you shall be clean . . . And I will put my spirit within you, and cause you to walk in my statutes . . .' (36:25, 27).

These two promises of God are in fact the two major blessings of that 'new covenant' which was predicted by Jeremiah. For the terms of the new covenant include these words: 'I will put my law within them, and I will write it upon their hearts. . . . I will forgive their iniquity, and I will remember their sin no more.'[3]

It is a wonderful witness to the unity of Scripture to see how the apostles took up these promises relating to the new covenant. They knew that the new covenant had now been established and ratified by the blood of Jesus (Mt. 26:28; Heb. 7:22; 8:1–13), and so they spoke freely of the availability through the same Lord Jesus of the promised blessings of the covenant. Thus Paul designated Christian ministers 'ministers of a new covenant' and went on at once to describe it as both 'the dispensation of righteousness'

---

[3] Je. 31:31–34. The writing of the law on the heart would of course be the work of the Holy Spirit, as is plain from Ezk. 36:27 and 2 Cor. 3:3, 6–8.

(*i.e.* justification) and 'the dispensation of the Spirit' (2 Cor. 3:6–9).

Similarly, the apostle Peter cried on the Day of Pentecost: 'Repent, and be baptized every one of you in the name of Jesus Christ for the forgiveness of your sins; and you shall receive the gift of the Holy Spirit' (Acts 2:38). Thus Peter assured all who would repent and believe,[4] and give public evidence of their penitent faith in Jesus by being baptized in his name, that they would receive from God two free gifts, namely the forgiveness of their sins and the gift of the Holy Spirit.

Moreover, a careful reading of the first two chapters of the Acts leads to the conclusion that this 'gift of the Spirit' is synonymous with what has earlier been termed 'the promise of the Spirit' (1:4; 2:33, 39), 'the baptism of the Spirit' (1:5) and 'the outpouring of the Spirit' (2:17, 33), although two of these expressions may be said to emphasize more the giving, and the other two more the receiving, of the Spirit. We could sum it up by saying that these penitent believers received the *gift* of the Spirit which God had *promised* before the Day of Pentecost, and were thus *baptized* with the Spirit whom God *poured out* on the Day of Pentecost. Further, the apostle Peter retained his conviction about this identification. When later Cornelius was converted and received the Spirit, he referred to this equally as the 'baptism' and as the 'gift' of the Spirit (Acts 11:16, 17).

In the light of all this biblical testimony it seems to me clear that the 'baptism' of the Spirit is the same as the promise or gift of the Spirit and is as much an integral part of the gospel of salvation as is the remission of sins. Certainly we must never conceive 'salvation' in purely negative terms, as if it consisted only of our rescue from sin, guilt, wrath and

---

[4] That faith was required in addition to repentance is plain from verse 41 'those who received his word' and verse 44 'all who believed', quite apart from the rest of the New Testament.

death. We thank God that it is all these things. But it also includes the positive blessing of the Holy Spirit to regenerate, indwell, liberate and transform us. What a truncated gospel we preach if we proclaim the one without the other! And what a glorious gospel we have to share when we are true to Scripture! When sinners repent and believe, Jesus not only takes away their sins but also baptizes them with his Spirit. Indeed, as Paul put it in dramatic terms to Titus, when God 'saves' us he not only 'justifies' us by his grace but also gives us a certain 'washing' or 'bath'. If, as is probable, this is a reference to water-baptism, then it indicates what water-baptism signifies. For Paul describes it by a remarkable, composite expression. It is a 'bath of rebirth and renewal of (*i.e.* by) the Holy Spirit whom he abundantly poured out upon us through Jesus Christ our Saviour' (3:4–7, literally). So the outpoured Spirit to regenerate and renew us is again seen to be part of our salvation. The 'baptism' or 'gift' of the Spirit is indeed one of the distinctive blessings of the new age ushered in by Jesus Christ.

The promise of a universal blessing

The next step in our argument is to see that the outpouring or baptism of the Spirit is not only a *distinctive* blessing of the new age (in that it was not available previously) but also a *universal* blessing (in that it is now the birthright of all God's children). This has already become apparent from the fact that it is part of the salvation which God gives us through Christ. But there are other evidences which confirm it.

The first is Joel's prophecy and Peter's understanding of it. The emphasis in God's promise through Joel is on the universality of the gift of the Spirit. Here are the terms in which Peter quoted it: 'And in the last days it shall be, God declares, that I will pour out my Spirit upon all flesh' (Acts 2:17). This cannot mean 'all flesh' irrespective of their inward readiness to receive the gift, their repentance and faith, but rather 'all flesh' irrespective of their outward status and privilege. It indicates that there is to be no distinction of sex or age, of rank or race, in the reception of this divine gift, for both sons and daughters, young men and old men, menservants and maidservants, and even 'all that are far off' (verse 39), which means the Gentiles, are to receive it. Further, out of every age, sex, race and rank it includes *all* who repent and believe.

In Old Testament days, although all believers were indeed regenerate,[5] the Holy Spirit came upon special people for special ministries at special times. He still does endue special men for special tasks, as we shall see. But now his ministry is wider and deeper than ever it was in Old Testament days. What, then, is the difference between his ministry in Old Testament days and his ministry today? First, all believers of all flesh now share in the blessing of the Spirit. Secondly, although Old Testament believers knew God and experienced a new birth, there is now an indwelling of the Spirit which they never knew, which belongs to the new covenant and the kingdom of God, and which both the prophets and the Lord Jesus promised (Je. 31:33; Ezk. 36:26, 27; Jn. 14:16, 17; Rom. 14:17). Thirdly, the Holy Spirit's distinctive work now relates essentially to Jesus Christ. We saw earlier that in his sanctifying ministry he reveals Christ to believers and forms Christ in believers, and this, in the nature of the case, he could not have done before Christ came (*e.g.* Jn. 16:14; Gal. 4:19; Eph. 3:16, 17).

That Peter understood the Joel prophecy to promise this gift or baptism of the Spirit to all believers seems clear from the conclusion of his great sermon (Acts 2:38, 39), in which

[5] The chief evidences for this are indirect. First, they were certainly 'justified' (*cf.* Rom. 4:1-8, based on Gn. 15:6 and Ps. 32:1, 2), and it is difficult to conceive how a sinner can be justified without being regenerate. Secondly, they claimed to love God's law (*e.g.* Ps. 119:97). Since the unregenerate nature is hostile to God and resistant to his law (Rom. 8:7), they seem to have possessed a new nature. We sing the Psalms in Christian worship because we recognize in them the language of the regenerate.

he applied it to his hearers: 'Repent, and be baptized every one of you in the name of Jesus Christ for the forgiveness of your sins; and you shall receive the gift of the Holy Spirit. For the promise (*i.e.* which we have inherited, see verse 33) is to you (as well as to us) and to your children and to all that are far off, every one whom the Lord our God calls to him.' This last phrase is a very clear and striking assertion. It is that the promise of the 'gift' or 'baptism' of the Spirit is to as many as the Lord our God calls. The promise of God is co-extensive with the call of God. Whoever receives the divine call inherits the divine promise.

The Day of Pentecost

And this is what happened! Three thousand of those who heard the word that day repented, believed and were baptized with water. And although we are not specifically told that they received the remission of sins and the gift of the Spirit, yet the strong presumption is that they did. This is not a precarious argument from silence. It is based on the unequivocal promise of the apostle Peter that they would receive these gifts if they repented, believed and were baptized. We are told that they were baptized (verse 41), having 'received his word' (*i.e.* with penitent faith). Since they thus fulfilled the conditions, God must have fulfilled his promise. This means that, according to the second chapter of Acts, two separate companies of people received the 'baptism' or 'gift' of the Spirit on the Day of Pentecost – the 120 at the beginning of the chapter, and the 3,000 at the end.

The 3,000 do not seem to have experienced the same miraculous phenomena (the rushing mighty wind, the tongues of flame, or the speech in foreign languages). At least nothing is said about these things. Yet because of God's assurance through Peter they must have inherited the same promise and received the same gift (verses 33, 39). Nevertheless, there was this difference between them: the 120 were regenerate already, and received the baptism of the

Spirit only after waiting upon God for ten days. The 3,000 on the other hand were unbelievers, and received the forgiveness of their sins and the gift of the Spirit simultaneously – and it happened immediately they repented and believed, without any need to wait.

This distinction between the two companies, the 120 and the 3,000, is of great importance, because the *norm* for today must surely be the second group, the 3,000, and not (as is often supposed) the first. The fact that the experience of the 120 was in two distinct stages was due simply to historical circumstances. They could not have received the Pentecostal gift before Pentecost. But those historical circumstances have long since ceased to exist. We live after the event of Pentecost, like the 3,000. With us, therefore, as with them, the forgiveness of sins and the 'gift' or 'baptism' of the Spirit are received together.

This is not to say that everything connected with the second group on the Day of Pentecost is normative for Christian experience today. I think it will be agreed that the ingathering of 3,000 converts as the result of a single sermon was a bit exceptional; it is certainly not the average expectation of an evangelist in the modern world!

The truth is that the Day of Pentecost had at least two distinct meanings, and a failure to grasp the distinction between them lies at the root of much modern confusion. In the first place, it was the last event of the saving career of Jesus, the long-promised outpouring of the Spirit consequent upon his death, resurrection and ascension. As such it completed the inauguration of the new or Messianic age, the age of the Spirit. In itself it is unrepeatable, as unrepeatable as the Saviour's death, resurrection and ascension which preceded it. But its blessings are for all who belong to Christ. All Christians since that day, without any exception, have become participants in this new age and have received the gifts of forgiveness and the Spirit which Christ made available by his death, resurrection, ascension and outpouring of the Spirit. In this sense those converted on the Day of Pentecost as a result of Peter's sermon were typical of all subsequent believers.

But the Day of Pentecost had another and more unusual meaning. It was the fulfilment not only of the general Old Testament expectation of the Spirit's coming, but also of those special promises of Jesus in the Upper Room which were addressed primarily to the apostles and whose fulfilment was intended to equip them for their particular apostolic work as inspired and authoritative teachers.

Pentecost may also have a third significance. It may rightly be considered the first 'revival', the first time the Spirit put forth his power in such an abundant measure that as many as 3,000 were simultaneously convicted of sin, born again and welcomed into the Christian community. Such revivals or unusual manifestations of the Spirit's power have continued in the history of the Christian church from time to time. But they cannot be regarded as a norm.

What was normative, however, was the experience specifically promised in Peter's conclusion to *all* whom God calls and who respond in penitent faith, namely that they would receive both forgiveness and the Holy Spirit. These two gifts were and still are bestowed and received together. There is no interval between them as there had been (for the exceptional historical reason explained above) in the case of the 120.

Some readers may immediately object that the 120 were not unique, since the experience of certain Samaritan believers and of some disciples of John the Baptist, recorded later in the Acts (8:5–17 and 19:1–7), was in two stages also. We shall look at these two passages in a moment. Meanwhile, I must first repeat that a doctrine of the Holy Spirit must not be constructed from purely descriptive passages in the Acts. It would be impossible to build a consistent doctrine from them because there is no consistency about them. You cannot even derive a doctrine of the Holy

Spirit from the *description* of the Day of Pentecost; what I have attempted above is some deductions from the *interpretations* of the event which Peter gave in his sermon. Further, it is a fundamental principle of biblical interpretation to begin with the general, not the special. The essential question to ask is what is the general teaching of the New Testament authors regarding the reception of the Holy Spirit. We shall then be in a position to consider in the light of this general teaching both apparent deviations from this norm and the narrative portions of the Acts.

What, then, did the apostles teach about when and how the Holy Spirit is received? To this question we can give a plain and definite answer. We have just observed what Peter taught. Now consider that Paul consistently taught the same thing. We 'receive the Spirit', he insisted, not as a result of any good works of obedience which we may have done, but 'by hearing with faith', that is, by hearing and believing the gospel (Gal. 3:2). More simply, 'we . . . receive the promise of the Spirit through faith' (Gal. 3:14). And the context makes it clear that this 'faith' is not some second, post-conversion act of faith, but saving faith, the faith which responds to the gospel and lays hold of Christ.

The Samaritan believers
Having grasped the plain, general teaching of Jesus and his apostles that the gift or baptism of the Holy Spirit is a universal blessing, the common possession of all the children of God, we are ready to come back to the two passages in the Acts in which we meet people who appear to have become believers without receiving the Holy Spirit. As we study them carefully, we shall not fail to observe that there is something unusual, something irregular, about both situations.

The first is Acts 8:5–17. Philip the evangelist has preached the gospel in Samaria, and many have believed and been

31

baptized. There can be little, if any, doubt that they were genuine Christian believers; no hint is given that their response had been defective. The only exception was Simon Magus, who is said to have 'believed' (verse 13), but whose profession of faith turned out later to have been spurious (verses 20–23). The first sign that anything is unusual about this incident is that 'when the apostles at Jerusalem heard that Samaria had received the word of God, they sent to them Peter and John' (verse 14). Why? There is no evidence that on other occasions evangelistic work had to be inspected or vetted by two apostles. For example, at the end of the same chapter (verses 26–40) the same Philip preached the gospel to an Ethiopian eunuch and baptized him when he believed. But no apostle was sent to investigate or to lay hands on him. What then is the explanation of this exceptional procedure of an apostolic delegation?

The most probable answer is not just that this was the first time the gospel had been preached outside Jerusalem (verses 1, 4), but that these converts were Samaritans. This is certainly the importance of the story in Luke's account of the unfolding Christian mission. He is describing how Jesus' pre-Pentecost command came to be fulfilled: 'you shall be my witnesses in Jerusalem and in all Judea and Samaria and to the end of the earth' (1:8). Philip's decision to proclaim Christ to the Samaritans (8:5) was a very bold step to have taken. For centuries there had been bitter rivalry between Jews and Samaritans, and still at that time the Jews had 'no dealings with Samaritans' (Jn. 4:9). But now not only had a Jew preached to Samaritans, but Samaritans had accepted the Jew's message! What would happen? It was an exciting moment, and a dangerous one too. Was Philip right to have taken this step? Could Samaritans really have embraced the gospel? And, more important, would they be acceptable to Jewish believers? Or would the ancient Jewish-Samaritan schism survive in the church and become a disastrous division between

Jewish Christians and Samaritan Christians? Is it not reasonable to suppose that it was precisely in order to avoid the development of such a situation that God deliberately withheld the gift of his Spirit from the Samaritan believers (or at least outward evidence of the gift) until two of the leading apostles came down to investigate and, by the laying on of their hands, acknowledged and confirmed the genuineness of the Samaritans' conversion? No other explanation of the Samaritan story (a) brings it into harmony with the apostles' general teaching, from which it deviates, and (b) at the same time sets it in its historical context.

Because this Samaritan incident was so clearly abnormal, it is difficult to see how most Pentecostal and some charismatic Christians can regard it as constituting a norm for spiritual experience today, namely that the Holy Spirit is given subsequently to conversion. It is equally difficult to justify the 'catholic' view that the Spirit is given only through the imposition of apostolic hands (which they understand as meaning the hands of bishops regarded as 'in the apostolic succession'). Is it not clear from the rest of the New Testament that both the timing and the means of the gift to the Samaritans were atypical? If so, then neither a two-stage experience nor the laying-on of hands is the norm for receiving the Spirit today. [6]

Some charismatics accept this argument about the norm, but come back with a counter-suggestion. Granted, they say, that the Samaritans' experience was abnormal; could not this abnormality be repeated sometimes today? Our answer to this question will be determined, I think, by our

[6] Episcopal 'Confirmation' is the way the Anglican church has chosen to receive into full church membership those who have been baptized (usually in infancy) and have themselves repented and believed. The laying-on of hands is a seemly biblical sign of blessing, but is not the normal means by which the Holy Spirit is given and received. The 1662 Book of Common Prayer implies no more than that God may use this sign, accompanied by the prayers of the congregation, to 'certify' the candidates of his favour towards them and to 'strengthen' them by the Holy Spirit.

understanding of the reasons for the Samaritan abnormality. If it could be shown that their original non-reception of the Spirit was due to their own defective grasp of the gospel or response to the gospel, then it could perhaps be argued that a similar defective response today might result in a similar defective initiation. But I do not think this can be shown. At least there is simply nothing in Luke's narrative to suggest either that Philip did not teach properly or that the Samaritans did not believe properly, so that the apostles had to supplement Philip's teaching or improve the Samaritans' understanding. On the contrary, what brought the apostles to Samaria was precisely the news that these people 'had received the word of God' (verse 14). There does not appear to have been anything faulty either in the Word of God which they heard or in the reception which they gave it. Instead, as has been urged above, the reason why the Spirit was not given seems to lie in the historical situation. And since this historical situation was unique and cannot be repeated (the Jewish-Samaritan schism having long since been swallowed up by the universal Christian mission), I cannot myself see how the abnormality in the Samaritan reception of the Spirit could be taken as a precedent for today.

The Ephesian disciples

The second unusual incident is described in Acts 19:1-7. Paul had begun the third of his famous missionary journeys and come to Ephesus. There he met about a dozen men who, if we may judge from Luke's description of them, do not seem to have been Christians at all. It is true that he calls them 'disciples' (verse 1), but this need mean no more than *professing* disciples, just as Simon Magus is said to have 'believed' (8:13), although the context indicates that he had only *professed* to believe. Commenting on a different passage of Scripture, Charles Hodge, the nineteenth-century Princeton scholar, wrote: 'the Scripture always speaks of men according to their profession, calling those who profess faith, believers, and those who confess Christ, Christians.'[7] Paul asked them if they received the Holy Spirit when they 'believed' (verse 2). This at least indicates that he knew they professed to be believers. But it also suggests that for some reason he doubted the reality of their faith or he would never have asked the question. He taught consistently, as we have seen, that the Spirit is given to believers; so how could he have asked his questions unless something made him suspicious of their Christian life and therefore of their profession of faith?

Events proved his suspicions correct. We may note these points: a. In answer to his question whether they had received the Spirit, they said neither a simple 'yes' or 'no', nor even a puzzled 'don't know', but 'we have never even heard that there is a Holy Spirit' (verse 2)! b. Then Paul immediately asked them about their baptism (verse 3), for water-baptism is in the name of the Trinity (Mt. 28:19) and, as will be shown, dramatizes Spirit-baptism. So how could they have received Christian baptism if they had never heard of the Holy Spirit? He was right. They had not been baptized. c. What they had received was John the Baptist's baptism, probably as a result of the incomplete teaching of Apollos who had just visited Ephesus (18:24–26). So what did Paul do? He did not go on to some higher or fuller teaching; he went right back to the beginning, to the very essence of the gospel. He explained that 'the one who was to come', in whom John the Baptist had told them to believe, was in fact 'Jesus' (verse 4). d. Paul then baptized them 'in the name of the Lord Jesus' and laid his hands on them, with the result that 'the Holy Spirit came upon them' with accompanying signs (languages and prophecy) as visible, audible evidence.

Now some teachers use this story to endorse their view

[7] C. Hodge, *A Commentary on the Epistle to the Ephesians*, 1856 (Banner of Truth, London, 1964), p. 124.

that in normal Christian experience the gift or baptism of the Spirit is a second and subsequent experience, following conversion. But the story really should not be used in this way. I am not, of course, denying that these men received the Spirit when Paul baptized them and laid his hands on them. But the question is: were they Christians before this? We have seen that they were in some sense professing 'disciples'. But is it seriously maintained that people who have never heard of the Holy Spirit, nor been baptized in the name of Jesus, nor even apparently believed in Jesus, were true Christian disciples? Surely not. If they were anybody's disciples, they were disciples of Apollos and of John the Baptist. They were not clearly converted Christians. They certainly cannot be regarded as typical of Christian believers today.

Other expositors draw attention to the sequence of events, namely belief in Jesus – baptism in the name of Jesus – the imposition of Paul's hands – the coming of the Holy Spirit. They emphasize that the Spirit came upon these Ephesians not only after they had believed but also after Paul had both baptized them and laid his hands on them. This is so; but I do not myself think the order is very significant. To me the really important point is that all four events belonged together and cannot be separated. They were different parts of a single initiation into Christ, which took place by both baptism and the laying-on of hands (outwardly) and by both faith and the gift of the Spirit (inwardly).

The language of baptism

What has emerged from our study so far, and is not negatived by the exceptional cases of Acts 8 and 19, is that the gift of the Holy Spirit is a *universal* Christian experience because it is an *initial* Christian experience. All Christians receive the Spirit at the very beginning of their Christian life.

This truth is further confirmed by the New Testament

use of the expression '*baptism* of the Spirit' as an equivalent to 'gift of the Spirit', or rather of the verb (for the expression is always verbal) to 'baptize' or 'be baptized' with the Holy Spirit. The very concept of 'baptism' is initiatory. Water-baptism is the public rite of initiation into Christ. It signifies visibly both the washing away of sin (Acts 22:16) and the bestowal of the Holy Spirit. See Acts 2:38, where both aspects of salvation are linked to baptism. It is the symbol of which Spirit-baptism is the reality. This must be why Peter's immediate reaction, when Cornelius was baptized with the Spirit, was to say: 'can anyone forbid water for baptizing these people who have received the Holy Spirit just as we have?' (Acts 10:47; 11:16). If they had received the reality, how could they be refused the sign? It also explains Paul's second question to those Ephesian 'disciples'. When they told him they had never even heard of the Holy Spirit, he at once asked into what they had been baptized. Both apostles clearly associated the two baptisms.

Moreover, there can be no doubt that Cornelius' baptism with the Spirit was his initiation into Christ, his conversion. He had been told by an angel of God to send for Simon Peter who would declare to him a message by which he and his household would be 'saved' (11:14). So Peter preached the gospel to him, ending with the promise of forgiveness of sins through the name of Jesus (10:43). After Cornelius and his household had believed (15:7), and been baptized both with the Spirit and with water, they are described as having 'received the word of God' (11:1), while (in two significant phrases) God is said to have both 'granted them repentance unto life' (11:18) and 'cleansed their hearts by faith' (15:9).

This recognition of the *initial* nature of the gift of the Spirit, as indicated by the term 'baptism' and illustrated by the conversion of Cornelius, is entirely in keeping with the general teaching of the apostles, as we have already considered. To be 'in the Spirit' (which in Pauline language is the same as to be 'in Christ'), to 'have' the Spirit, to 'live by

37

the Spirit' and to be 'led by the Spirit' – these are all descriptions of every Christian believer, however young in the faith he may be, indeed from the very moment of his new birth (Rom. 8:9; Gal. 5:25; Rom. 8:14). The New Testament authors take it for granted that God has 'given' their readers his Holy Spirit (*e.g.* Rom. 5:5; 1 Thes. 4:8; 1 Jn. 3:24; 4:13); there is no single occasion on which they exhort them to receive him.

1 Corinthians 12:13

Further confirmation that to 'be baptized with the Spirit' is initiatory comes from a comparison of the seven verses in which the expression occurs, and in particular from a study of the only one outside the Gospels and the Acts.

The first four uses of the expression are found in John the Baptist's descriptive prophecy of the ministry of the Lord Jesus: 'He will baptize with the Holy Spirit' (Mt. 3:11; Mk. 1:8; Lk. 3:16; Jn. 1:33). The fifth is our Lord's quotation of John's prophecy, in which he applies it to Pentecost: 'before many days you shall be baptized with the Holy Spirit' (Acts 1:5). The sixth is the apostle Peter's quotation of our Lord's quotation of John's prophecy, in which he applies it to the conversion of Cornelius, which we have just been considering. He tells the Jerusalem apostles and others: 'I remembered the word of the Lord, how he said, "John baptized with water, but you shall be baptized with the Holy Spirit" ' (Acts 11:16).

The seventh – and only other – occurrence of the expression is to be found in 1 Corinthians 12:13. Here Paul writes: 'For by one Spirit we were all baptized into one body – Jews or Greeks, slaves or free – and all were made to drink of one Spirit.' This cannot be a simple reference to the Day of Pentecost, for neither Paul nor the Corinthians were there to share in the event itself. Yet both he and they had come to share in the blessing which that event made possible. They had received the Holy Spirit, or rather, to use his own terminology, they had been 'baptized' with the Holy Spirit and had been 'made to drink' of the Holy Spirit.

What is immediately striking about this verse is the emphatic repetition of the word 'all' ('*all* baptized', '*all* ... made to drink') and the similarly emphatic repetition of the word 'one' ('by *one* Spirit', 'into *one* body', 'of *one* Spirit') with which it is deliberately contrasted. This is in keeping with the context. What the apostle is doing in 1 Corinthians 12 is to emphasize at the beginning of the chapter the *unity* of the Spirit, the giver of spiritual gifts, before he goes on in the second half of the chapter to unfold the *diversity* of the gifts themselves. He is underlining our common experience as Christian believers of the Holy Spirit. This is the difference between 'the gift of the Spirit' (meaning the Holy Spirit himself) and 'the gifts of the Spirit' (meaning the spiritual gifts which he distributes).

Three times in the first half of the chapter he writes (literally) of 'the one Spirit' (9b, 13a and b), three times of 'the same Spirit' (4, 8, 9a), and once of 'the one and the same Spirit' (11). This is his emphasis. His climax comes in verse 13: 'For by one Spirit we were all baptized into one body ... and all were made to drink of one Spirit.' So the baptism of the Spirit in this verse, far from being a dividing factor (some have it, others have not), is the great uniting factor (an experience we have all had). It is, in fact, the means of entry into the body of Christ. And Paul's mention of Jews and Greeks, slaves and free, may even be an allusion to Joel's 'all flesh', irrespective of race or rank. The oneness of the body is created by the oneness of the Spirit, which is exactly what Paul implies in Ephesians 4:4: 'There is one body and one Spirit.' It is difficult, then, to resist the conclusion that the baptism of the Spirit is not a second and subsequent experience enjoyed by some Christians, but the initial experience enjoyed by all.

Some do not accept this conclusion, however, but draw

a subtle exegetical distinction. They argue that, while the other six verses refer to a baptism by Jesus Christ in or with the Holy Spirit, the seventh verse (1 Cor. 12:13) refers to a baptism by the Holy Spirit into the body of Christ, and is therefore something quite different. 'The Holy Spirit has indeed baptized us all into the body of Christ,' they say, 'but this does not prove that Christ has baptized us all with the Holy Spirit.' To me this is an example of special pleading. The Greek expression is precisely the same in all its seven occurrences,[8] and therefore *a priori*, as a sound principle of interpretation, it should be taken to refer to the same baptism experience in each verse. The burden of proof rests with those who deny it. The natural interpretation is that Paul is echoing the words of John the Baptist as first Jesus and then Peter had done (Acts 1:5; 11:16). It is unnatural to make Jesus Christ the baptizer in six instances, and the Holy Spirit the baptizer in the seventh. I think we must even dissent from the RSV translation of 1 Corinthians 12:13, '*by* one Spirit we were all baptized . . .'. The Greek preposition in this verse is *en*, just as in the other six verses, where it is translated 'with'; why should it be rendered differently here? If it is because the words *en heni pneumati* (RSV 'by one Spirit') come at the beginning of the sentence, the reason for this is surely that Paul is stressing the oneness of the Spirit in whom we share, not that the Spirit is the baptizer.

Let me enlarge on my point in this way. In every kind of baptism (of water, blood, fire, Spirit, *etc.*) there are four parts. To begin with, there are the subject and the object, namely the baptizer and the baptized. Thirdly, there is the element with or in (*en*) which, and fourthly, there is the purpose for (*eis*) which, the baptism takes place. Take, as an example, the crossing of the Red Sea, which the apostle Paul describes as a kind of baptism (1 Cor. 10:1, 2). Pre-

---

[8] The only difference is that six times the Spirit is characterized as 'holy', and in the seventh verse as 'one'.

sumably God himself was the baptizer. Certainly the escaping Israelites were the baptized. The element in which the baptism was administered was water or spray from the cloud and the sea, while its purpose is indicated in the expression 'baptized into Moses', that is, into relationship with him as their God-appointed leader.

In John's baptism, John the Baptist was the subject, while the objects were the people of 'Jerusalem and all Judea and all the region about the Jordan' (Mt. 3:5). The baptism took place in (*en*) the waters of the River Jordan and was for or unto (*eis*) repentance (Mt. 3:11) and therefore the remission of sins (Mk. 1:4; Lk. 3:3).

Christian baptism is similar. The minister baptizes the professing believer with or in (*en*) water. And the baptism is into (*eis*) the one name of the Trinity (Mt. 28:19), or more precisely into the name of the Lord Jesus (Acts 8:16; 19:5), that is, into Christ crucified and risen (Rom. 6:3, 4).

It will be seen from these examples that in every kind of baptism there are not only a subject and an object, but also both an *en* and an *eis*, that is, both an element with or in which, and a purpose for which, the baptism is administered. The baptism of the Spirit is no exception. If we put the seven references to this baptism together, we learn that Jesus Christ is the baptizer, as John the Baptist clearly foretold. According to 1 Corinthians 12:13 the baptized are 'we all'. The Holy Spirit is himself the 'element' with, or in (*en*), which[9] the baptism takes place (if one may so describe the Third Person of the Trinity; the analogy between

---

[9] Pentecostal and charismatic Christians usually speak of 'baptism *in* the Spirit' rather than 'baptism *with* the Spirit'. The Greek preposition *en* may be translated either way. The expression chosen is likely to depend on whether one considers that water-baptism should be administered by immersion or by affusion. Those who practise immersion speak of baptism *in* the Spirit presumably because they think of the Spirit as the element in which one is plunged. Since, however, it is when the Holy Spirit is 'poured out' upon people that they are said to be 'baptized', 'baptism *with* the Spirit' seems to me preferable.

baptism with water and baptism with the Spirit seems to make it legitimate). And the purpose of this baptism is incorporation 'into (*eis*) one body', namely the body of Christ, the church.

It is quite true that of these four aspects of baptism the only one which is explicitly common to all seven verses is that this baptism is 'with (*en*) the Spirit'. Although all thus mention the 'element', not every verse specifies either the subject or the object or the purpose of the baptism. This should not surprise us, however, since the same omissions occur with New Testament references to water-baptism. It is sometimes argued that in 1 Corinthians 12:13 the Holy Spirit must be the baptizer, since otherwise the baptism would have no subject. But no baptizer is mentioned in Acts 1:5 and 11:16 either. We find no difficulty in supplying Jesus Christ as the baptizer in those verses; why should we not do the same in 1 Corinthians 12:13? The reason why Christ is not specifically mentioned as the baptizer in these three verses is not far to seek. It is that, whereas in the four Gospels the verb is in the active and Christ is its subject ('he will baptize', 'this is he who baptizes'), in these other three verses the verb is passive and the subject is those baptized ('you shall be baptized', 'we were all baptized'). The active verbs contrast John and Jesus as the two baptizers. When the verbs are passive, however, the identity of the baptizer fades, and the emphasis lies rather on either the favoured people who receive the baptism or the one Spirit with whom they are baptized. I reaffirm, therefore, that in 1 Corinthians 12:13, although he is not named, Jesus Christ must be regarded as the baptizer.

The argument rests partly on the six other verses in which the same expression occurs, and partly on the impossibility of the alternative. If 1 Corinthians 12:13 were different and in this verse the Holy Spirit were himself the baptizer, what would be the 'element' with which he baptizes? That there is no answer to this question seems enough to overthrow this interpretation, since the baptism metaphor absolutely requires an 'element'; otherwise the baptism is no baptism. Therefore, the 'element' in the baptism of 1 Corinthians 12:13 must be the Holy Spirit, and (consistently with the other verses) we must supply Jesus Christ as the baptizer. Similarly, at the end of the verse it is the Holy Spirit of whom we drink and (consistently with Jn. 7:37 ff.) it must be Christ by whom we are 'made to drink' of him.

Having tried to see that 1 Corinthians 12:13 refers to Christ baptizing with the Spirit and causing us to drink of the Spirit, we must note next that 'we all' have shared in this baptism and this drinking. The being baptized and the drinking are clearly equivalent expressions. All Christians have experienced them both. Moreover, the aorist tense of both verbs ('were ... baptized', 'were made to drink') must be taken as an allusion, not just to the Pentecost event, but also to its blessing personally received by all Christians at their conversion.

Conclusion

The evidence, then, which I have sought to gather from the New Testament in general, and in particular from Peter's sermon in Acts 2 and Paul's teaching in 1 Corinthians 12:13, indicates that the 'baptism' of the Spirit is identical with the 'gift' of the Spirit, that it is one of the *distinctive* blessings of the new covenant, and, because it is an *initial* blessing, is also a *universal* blessing for members of the covenant. It is part and parcel of belonging to the new age. The Lord Jesus, the mediator of the new covenant and the bestower of its blessings, gives both the forgiveness of sins and the gift of the Spirit to all who enter his covenant. Further, baptism with water is the sign and seal of baptism with the Spirit, as much as it is of the forgiveness of sins. Water-baptism is the initiatory Christian rite, because Spirit-baptism is the initiatory Christian experience. So then, whatever post-conversion experiences there may be (and I shall come to

43

them later), 'baptism with the Spirit' cannot be the right expression to use for them.

God's purpose is that all his people shall both receive the new covenant blessings of the forgiveness of sins and the gift of the Spirit, and receive water-baptism as the sign and seal of these blessings. They are then to continue to be filled with the Spirit and manifest this fullness in holiness of life and boldness of testimony. All Christians are described in the Epistle to the Hebrews as being 'partakers of the Holy Spirit', who have 'tasted . . . the powers of the age to come' (6:4, 5). The whole Christian life according to the New Testament is life in the Spirit following birth of the Spirit.

Moreover, the overwhelming emphasis of the New Testament letters is not to urge upon Christian readers some entirely new and distinct blessing, but to remind us of what by grace we are, to recall us to it, and to urge us to live by it. This is a very important point and not sufficiently grasped. The horizons of some Christians seem to be bounded by a second and subsequent experience which they call 'baptism in the Spirit'. In conversation with them, if they think you have had it, then this is what they are looking back to, and this is the chief bond which unites you. If, on the other hand, they think you have not had it, then this is what they are looking forward to, and this is the chief longing they have for you. So whether they are looking to the past or the future, it is 'the baptism of the Spirit' as a second experience which fills their horizon. But I have to say, really without any fear of possible contradiction, that this is *never* the perspective of the New Testament authors. When they are looking back, they are recalling that great act which God performed when he put us in Christ, justified, redeemed, regenerated and recreated us. To that they constantly appeal. And when they are looking forward, it is to their readers' growth into maturity and, beyond that, to the perfection which awaits the glorious appearing of the Saviour.

For example, when the apostle John handles in his first letter the necessity and the possibility of holiness, to what does he relate it? Not to a special 'baptism of the Spirit' which his readers either have had or should have, but to their original birth of God and to their duty to abide in Christ. Thus, 'No one born of God commits (or practises) sin . . . and he cannot sin (or continue in sin) because he is born of God.' Again, 'We know that any one born of God does not sin (or go on sinning)' (1 Jn. 3:9; 5:18).

What, next, are the apostles looking forward to? They urge upon us ethical conduct, often in considerable detail. They appeal to us to live out in the concrete realities of daily life what God has already done for us in Christ. They command us to grow in faith, love, knowledge and holiness. They warn us of judgment and challenge us with the expectation of the Lord's return. Meanwhile, they beg us not to grieve the Spirit, but rather to walk in the Spirit and to go on being filled with the Spirit, as we shall see in the next chapter. But never, not once, do they exhort and instruct us to 'be baptized with the Spirit'. There can be only one explanation of this, namely that they are writing to Christians, and Christians have already been baptized with the Holy Spirit.

This is not a mere argument about words, but about doctrine. The fundamental truth which is involved is that, by uniting us to Christ, God has given us everything. By the unutterable grace of God we have already been 'blessed . . . in Christ with every spiritual blessing' (Eph. 1:3), and our responsibility is constantly and progressively to appropriate these blessings which are already ours in Christ.

Similarly, since in Christ 'the whole fullness of deity dwells bodily', therefore if we are ourselves in Christ we 'have come to fullness of life in him' (Col. 2:9, 10). If God has given us the Lord Jesus Christ in his fullness, and if Christ already dwells within us by his Spirit, what more can God possibly add? Is not the very suggestion that there is some additional gift still to come derogatory to the fullness and the satisfactoriness of Jesus? Growth in Christ, yes! Additions to Christ, never! Thus, we have been begotten of God, we are his sons and heirs, we have died and risen with Christ, our bodies are the temples of the Holy Spirit (1 Cor. 6:19), and this indwelling Spirit is the guarantee, even the first-fruits, of our eternal inheritance in heaven. So what the New Testament authors constantly do is to remind us of our Christian privileges, in order to exhort us to lead a life that is worthy and appropriate. It is because of what we already are in Christ (God's children) and because of what we shall be when he appears (like him) that we are incited to be what we should be (pure as he is pure). See 1 John 3:1-3.

2 The Fullness of the Spirit

In the first chapter I have concentrated on the meaning of the expressions 'gift' or 'baptism' of the Spirit. I have tried to summarize the strong biblical evidence both that these two are one and the same thing, and that they describe an *initial* blessing (received at the beginning of the Christian life) not a subsequent one (received some time later), and therefore a *universal* blessing (given to all Christians) not an esoteric one (enjoyed only by some).

It may seem to some readers that this is an unhelpfully negative approach, and a sterile position as well, because it appears only to hark back to past experience and not to hold out any very exciting prospects for future Christian living. But this is not so. In turning our attention from the 'baptism' of the Spirit to the 'fullness' of the Spirit, we are turning from the initial gift God has given to all his children and will never take away to a condition which God intends to be continuous, but which may fluctuate. When we speak of the baptism of the Spirit we are referring to a once-for-all gift; when we speak of the fullness of the Spirit we are acknowledging that this gift needs to be *continuously and increasingly appropriated*.

The difference between 'baptism' and 'fullness'

Let me seek to elaborate what I have tried to show earlier. What happened on the Day of Pentecost was that Jesus 'poured out' the Spirit from heaven and thus 'baptized' with the Spirit first the 120 and then the 3,000. The result of this baptism of the Spirit was that 'they were all filled with the Holy Spirit' (Acts 2:4). Thus, the fullness of the Spirit was the consequence of the baptism of the Spirit. The baptism is what Jesus did (pouring out the Spirit from heaven); the fullness is what they received. The baptism was a unique initiatory experience; the fullness was intended to be the continuing, the permanent result, the norm. As an initiatory event the baptism is not repeatable and cannot be lost, but the filling can be repeated and in any case needs to be maintained. If it is not maintained, it is lost. If it is lost, it can be recovered. The Holy Spirit is 'grieved' by sin (Eph. 4:30) and ceases to fill the sinner. Repentance is then the only road to recovery. Even in cases where there is no suggestion that the fullness has been forfeited through sin, we still read of people being filled again, as a fresh crisis or challenge demands a fresh empowering by the Spirit.

A comparison of the various New Testament texts which speak of people being 'filled with' or 'full of' the Holy Spirit suggests that they fall into three main categories. First, it is implied that to be 'full' or 'filled' was a normal characteristic of every dedicated Christian. Thus, the seven who were set apart for the care of the Jerusalem widows were to be 'full of the Holy Spirit', as they were also to be 'of good repute', 'full of wisdom' and 'full of faith' (Acts 6:3, 5). Now I suppose their 'wisdom' and 'faith' might be regarded as special spiritual gifts. But a good reputation can hardly have been unusual for Christians. Nor, I think, was their being full of the Spirit. Similarly, Barnabas is described as 'a good man, full of the Holy Spirit and of faith' (Acts 11:24), and the newly-converted disciples of Pisidian

Antioch were 'filled with joy and with the Holy Spirit' (Acts 13:52). These verses appear to denote Christian normality, or at any rate what God intends Christian normality to be.

Secondly, the expression indicates an endowment for a particular ministry or office. Thus, John the Baptist would be 'filled with the Holy Spirit, even from his mother's womb' in preparation, it seems, for his prophetic ministry (Lk. 1:15–17). So, too, Ananias' words to Saul of Tarsus that he would be 'filled with the Holy Spirit' seem to allude to his appointment as an apostle (Acts 9:17; *cf.* 22:12–15 and 26:16–23).

Thirdly, there are occasions when the fullness of the Spirit was given to equip people not so much for lifelong office (*e.g.* as apostle or prophet) as for an immediate task, especially in an emergency. Zechariah was filled before he broke into prophecy (though his office was that of a priest, not a prophet. *Cf.* also his wife Elizabeth, Lk. 1:5–8, 41, 67). In the same way Peter before he addressed the Sanhedrin; the Christian group in Jerusalem before they continued their ministry of the word in spite of the onset of persecution; Stephen before he was martyred and Paul before he rebuked Elymas the magician – all these, we read, were 'filled with the Holy Spirit', presumably to empower them for the responsible task with which they were just then faced (Acts 4:8, 31; 7:55; 13:9).

This leaves Luke's very interesting fourfold reference to the Holy Spirit, in chapter 4 of his Gospel, in connection with the beginning of our Lord's public ministry. This seems to put his experience of the Spirit's fullness into all three categories. We are told that he returned from the Jordan 'full of the Holy Spirit', and we naturally assume that this was his invariable spiritual state. At the same time, the statement immediately follows his baptism at which the Spirit descended upon him (3:22) to 'anoint' and equip him for his ministry as the Messiah (4:14, 18). Thirdly,

49

since the story of the temptation is both introduced and concluded by references to the Holy Spirit (4:1, 'led by the Spirit' and 4:14, 'in the power of the Spirit') it seems that the Lord was specially strengthened by the Spirit for that emergency.

In addition to these varied descriptions of people being filled with the Spirit, either as a constant experience or for a specific purpose, Ephesians 5:18 contains the well-known command to all Christian people to be filled, that is, to go on being filled (a continuous present imperative) with the Spirit. We shall study this text in greater depth later.

There are no similar statements or commands in the New Testament about the baptism of the Spirit. The reason for this, I have suggested, is its initiatory character. No apostolic sermon or letter contains an appeal to be baptized with the Spirit. Indeed, all seven New Testament references to baptism with the Spirit are in the indicative, whether aorist, present or future; none is an exhortation in the imperative. The fact, however, that there are these references to the fullness of the Spirit, both describing how certain Christians were filled again, and commanding all Christians to go on being filled, shows that it is possible, and all too pitifully common, for Christians who have been baptized with the Spirit to cease to be filled with the Spirit.

The Corinthian Christians are a solemn warning to us on this score. It is plain from Paul's first letter to them that they had been baptized, all of them, with the Holy Spirit (12:13). They had also been enriched with all spiritual gifts (1:4–7). Yet the apostle rebukes them as *unspiritual* people, that is, as being not Spirit-filled. He makes it clear that the evidence of the Spirit's fullness is not the exercise of his gifts (of which they had plenty), but the ripening of his fruit (of which they had little). We shall consider in the next chapter what is meant by 'the fruit of the Spirit'. He could not address them, he writes, as *pneumatikoi*, 'spiritual' Christians, but only as *sarkinoi* or *sarkikoi*, 'carnal' Christians, even babes in Christ. Their carnality or immaturity was both intellectual and moral. It was revealed in their childish understanding on the one hand and in their jealousy and strife on the other (1 Cor. 3:1–4). They had been *baptized* with the Spirit, and richly *gifted* by the Spirit, but they were not (at least at the time of his visit and letter to them) *filled* with the Spirit. The apostle's distinction, you notice, is not between those who have received the baptism of the Spirit and those who have not, but between 'spiritual' Christians and 'carnal' Christians, that is, Christians filled with the Spirit and Christians dominated by the flesh. Is not the condition of the Corinthian Christians the condition of many of us today? We should not deny that, according to Scripture, we have been baptized with the Spirit because we have repented and believed, and our water-baptism has signified and sealed our Spirit-baptism. But are we filled with the Spirit? That is the question.

Many people would be unable to answer this question. They know neither whether they are filled with the Spirit nor how it is possible to tell. And when they come across the teaching that 'speaking in tongues' is the indispensable sign of having received the Spirit, they conclude that they have never received him, or at least his fullness. But it cannot be maintained from Scripture that 'tongues' always follow the reception of the Spirit. Of all the groups who received the Spirit in the book of Acts only three are said to have 'spoken in tongues' (2:1–4; 10:44–46; 19:1–6). Since the other people and groups who received the Spirit are not said to have done so, it would be arbitrary to assert that they did. Besides, the apostle categorically teaches in 1 Corinthians 12 that the gift of 'tongues' is only one of many gifts, which not all Christians are given; and there seems to be no solid foundation for the distinction some have tried to draw between the references to 'tongues' in Acts and those in 1 Corinthians 12 and 14, the former referring to the 'sign' of tongues which all must have and the latter to the 'gift' of tongues which only some receive. Indeed, several leaders of Pentecostal churches and of the charismatic movement are themselves now conceding that 'tongues' are not an indispensable sign of the gift of the Spirit. More will be said about this when we consider 'the gifts of the Spirit' in chapter 4.

What then is the evidence of the Spirit's fullness? And how may his fullness be enjoyed? In order to answer these questions we shall first look at two crucial New Testament passages – the first coming from the lips of Jesus and the second from the pen of Paul – and then give some consideration to two contemporary problems relating to this New Testament teaching.

Continuous appropriation

The first passage emphasizes that in order to keep on being filled with the Holy Spirit we have to keep on coming to the Lord Jesus. I am referring to his own stirring words which are recorded in John 7:37–39 and which have been (and remain) a great help to me: 'On the last day of the feast, the great day, Jesus stood up and proclaimed, "If any one thirst, let him come to me and drink. He who believes in me, as the scripture has said, 'Out of his heart shall flow rivers of living water.'"' Now this', John comments, 'he said about the Spirit, which those who believed in him were to receive; for as yet the Spirit had not been given, because Jesus was not yet glorified.' 'It has been said', wrote Bishop J. C. Ryle, 'that there are some passages in Scripture which deserve to be printed in letters of gold. Of such passages the verses before us form one.'

It was the last day of the Feast of Tabernacles (verse 2), the climax of its seven days. One of the colourful rituals of the festival was that every morning a solemn procession, headed by a priest carrying a golden pitcher, went to fetch water from the Pool of Siloam and then poured it out as a libation on the west side of the altar. It seems to have been generally understood that this ceremony not only commemorated God's miraculous provision in the wilderness, but also symbolized the future outpouring of the Spirit promised through the prophet Joel. Jesus took this ritual as his text. He stood forth dramatically in some prominent place (he usually sat to teach, like the Rabbis), and loudly proclaimed that he himself would give to those who came to him both water to drink and water to flow.

What did he mean? He combined two vivid pictures. The first is of a tired and thirsty traveller in a hot climate. The sun beats down mercilessly upon him. His water-supply has run out. His mouth is dry, his lips parched, his face flushed, his whole body dehydrated. He pants for water to quench his thirst. He represents every person who is separated in any degree from Christ. The second picture is of a thirsty land. The tropical sun has baked the ground hard. The river-beds are dry. Trees and shrubs are shrivelled. Animals groan because there is no pasture. The land thirsts for water. This is the world, secular society without God, dessicated, dissatisfied, thirsty.

What, then, is the water? John tells us: 'this he said about the Spirit.' And John adds that 'as yet the Spirit had not been given'. His actual words, literally translated, are 'the Spirit was not yet'. This can mean neither that the Spirit was non-existent nor that he was inactive, but rather that he had not yet been poured out in Pentecostal fullness, in 'rivers of living water'. So the living water to quench the thirst of the weary traveller and to irrigate the parched world is the fullness of the Holy Spirit.

And how do we experience this invigorating, refreshing, thirst-quenching fullness? The answer is: 'Let him come to me and drink. He who believes in me. . . .' The phrases are two, but the condition is one. There is no difference between coming to Jesus and believing in him, for coming to him to drink is coming to him in faith. Now the verbs (thirsting, coming, drinking, believing) are all in the present tense. So we are not only to come to Jesus once, in penitence and faith, but also thereafter to keep coming and to keep drinking, because we keep thirsting. We do this physically. Whenever we are thirsty, we get a drink. We must learn to do it spiritually also. The Christian is a spiritual dipsomaniac, always thirsty, always drinking. And drinking is not asking for water, but actually taking it. It is extremely simple. Drinking is one of the first activities which babies learn; indeed they do it by instinct.

Then drinking water becomes flowing water. We cannot contain the Spirit we receive. As William Temple wrote: 'No one can possess (or rather be indwelt by) the Spirit of God and keep that Spirit to himself. Where the Spirit is, he flows forth; if there is no flowing forth, he is not there.' We must beware of any claim to the fullness of the Spirit which does not lead to an evangelistic concern and outreach. Moreover, notice the disparity between the water we drink in and the water that flows out. We can drink only small gulps, but as we keep coming, drinking, believing, so by the mighty operation of the Holy Spirit within us, our little sips are multiplied into a mighty confluence of flowing streams: 'rivers of living water' will flow out from within us. This is the spontaneous outflow from Spirit-filled Christians to the blessing of others. But there is no way to ensure a constant inflow and a constant outflow, except to keep coming to Jesus and to keep drinking. For the fullness of the Spirit is to be continuously appropriated by faith.

Marks of the Spirit's fullness

The second New Testament passage emphasizes the evidence of the Spirit's fullness, although it also contains a command to be filled, which we shall need to study carefully. What are the marks of a person filled with the Spirit of God today? There can be no doubt that the chief evidence is moral not miraculous, and lies in the Spirit's fruit not the

Spirit's gifts. We have already noted that the Corinthians, who had been baptized with the Spirit and had been endowed richly with the gifts of the Spirit, yet showed that they were 'unspiritual' Christians by their lack of the moral quality of love (1 Cor. 3:1-4). They proudly laid claim to a certain fullness, so that Paul could write to them with a touch of sarcasm 'already you are filled!' (4:8), but it was not the fullness of the Holy Spirit. If they had been filled with the Spirit, they would of course have been filled with love, the Spirit's first fruit. Love is the strong bond between the fruit and the gifts of the Spirit. This is not only because gifts without love are valueless (1 Cor. 13), but also because love desires gifts as a necessary equipment for the service of others.

In the one and only place in his letters in which the apostle Paul describes the consequences of the Spirit's fullness, they are all moral qualities. This passage is Ephesians 5:18-21:

> 'And do not get drunk with wine, for that is debauchery; but be filled with the Spirit, addressing one another in psalms and hymns and spiritual songs, singing and making melody to the Lord with all your heart, always and for everything giving thanks in the name of our Lord Jesus Christ to God the Father. Be subject to one another out of reverence for Christ.'

In the Greek text this paragraph consists of two verbs in the imperative ('do not get drunk with wine ... but be filled with the Spirit'), on which depend four verbs which are present participles (literally 'speaking', 'singing and making melody', 'giving thanks' and 'submitting'). That is, the single command to be filled with the Spirit is followed by four descriptive consequences of the Holy Spirit's fullness.

The command to be filled is placed in vivid contrast to the other command not to get drunk. Some people have too readily deduced from this that drunkenness and the fullness

55

of the Spirit are comparable. The fullness of the Spirit, they say, is a kind of spiritual inebriation, and what the apostle is doing is to set over against each other two intoxicated states, physical through wine and spiritual through the Spirit's fullness. This is not so. It is true that a drunken man is 'under the influence' of alcohol, and that similarly a Spirit-filled believer may be described as under the control of the Spirit. It is also true that on the Day of Pentecost, when the 120 spoke publicly in other languages as the Spirit gave them utterance, the reaction of some in the crowd was to comment, 'they are filled with new wine' (Acts 2:13). But those who said this were evidently a minority who supposed the disciples to be drunk because they could not understand any of the languages spoken, whereas the reaction of the majority was astonishment that the Galilean disciples were speaking intelligibly in the native languages of Asia and Africa which the crowd could understand.

It is a great mistake to suppose, therefore, that those first Spirit-filled believers were in a kind of drunken stupor, or that such a state is intended to be a pattern for all future experience of the Spirit's fullness. The opposite is the case. There is a clear implication in Ephesians 5:18 that drunkenness and the Spirit's fullness are not comparable in this respect, for drunkenness is branded as 'excess' (AV) or 'debauchery' (RSV). The Greek word *asōtia*, which in its two other New Testament occurrences means 'profligacy' (Tit. 1:6; 1 Pet. 4:4), literally describes a condition in which a person cannot 'save' or control himself. It is because drunkenness involves a loss of self-control, Paul writes, that it is to be avoided. It is implied that the contrasting state, the fullness of the Spirit, involves no loss of self-control. On the contrary, we are distinctly told in Galatians 5:23 that a part of the fruit of the Spirit is self-control (*enkrateia*)! The consequences of the fullness of the Spirit, as the apostle goes on to portray them, are to be found in intelligent, controlled, healthy relationships with God and with each other.

We can indeed agree that in both drunkenness and the fullness of the Spirit two strong influences are at work within us, alcohol in the bloodstream and the Holy Spirit in our hearts. But, whereas excessive alcohol leads to unrestrained and irrational licence, transforming the drunkard into an animal, the fullness of the Spirit leads to restrained and rational moral behaviour, transforming the Christian into the image of Christ. Thus, the results of being under the influence of spirits on the one hand and of the Holy Spirit of God on the other are totally and utterly different. One makes us like beasts, the other like Christ.

We are now in a position to look at the four wholesome results, and thereby solid objective evidences, of the fullness of the Spirit. These results are seen in relationships. The Spirit's fullness involves not a private, mystical experience so much as moral relationships with God and our fellow men.

The first is 'speaking'. According to the AV, it is 'speaking to yourselves'. This does not mean that those who are filled with the Spirit start talking to themselves as if their minds had come unhinged! The RSV is certainly correct in rendering the expression 'addressing one another'. In the parallel passage in Colossians (3:16) the apostle urges his readers to let the Word of Christ dwell in them richly so that they may 'teach and admonish one another in all wisdom'.

It is very striking that the first evidence of being filled with the Spirit is that we speak to each other. Yet it is not surprising, since the first fruit of the Spirit is love. However deep and intimate our communion with God may seem, we cannot claim the fullness of the Spirit if we are not on speaking terms with any of our fellows. The first sign of fullness is fellowship. Moreover, it is a spiritual fellowship, for we address one another not in worldly chit-chat but in 'psalms and hymns and spiritual songs'. This cannot of course mean that the normal method of communication between Spirit-filled believers is song! It means rather that true fellowship is expressed in common worship. A good example is the *Venite* (Ps. 95), which Anglicans often sing in public worship on Sunday morning. Strictly speaking, it is not a psalm of worship at all. For it is not addressed to God but to the congregation: 'O come, let us sing unto the Lord.' Here are God's people addressing one another in a psalm, exhorting one another to worship their Lord.

This leads to the second result of the Spirit's fullness, which is 'singing and making melody' to the Lord. The Holy Spirit loves to glorify the Lord Jesus, manifesting him to his people in such a way that they delight to sing his praises. Unmusical people have sometimes taken comfort from the AV rendering of this exhortation which is to sing to the Lord 'in your heart'. For this phraseology suggests that their jubilation may be entirely inward, intended only 'for the ears of the Lord' (J. B. Phillips)! But the RSV is probably right to translate the expression 'with all your heart'. The heart indicates not so much the place as the manner in which we are to sing. The apostle exhorts us not to silent, but to heartfelt, worship.

Thirdly, we are to be 'always and for everything giving thanks'. Most of us give thanks sometimes for some things; Spirit-filled believers give thanks always for all things. There is no time at which, and no circumstance for which, they do not give thanks. They do so 'in the name of our Lord Jesus Christ', that is, because they are one with Christ, and 'to God the Father', because the Holy Spirit witnesses with their spirit that they are God's children and that their Father is wholly good and wise. Grumbling, one of Irsael's besetting sins, is serious because it is a symptom of unbelief. Whenever we start moaning and groaning, it is proof positive that we are not filled with the Spirit. Whenever the Holy Spirit fills believers, they thank their heavenly Father at all times for all things.

We have seen that the second and third marks of the

Spirit's fullness are both Godward – singing to the Lord and giving thanks to the Father. The Holy Spirit puts us into a right and praising relationship with the Father and the Son. The Spirit-filled believer has no practical difficulties with the doctrine of the Trinity. The first and fourth marks, however, concern our relationship with each other, speaking to one another and now submitting to one another.

Although the apostle goes on to show that submission is the *particular* duty of a wife to her husband, children to their parents and servants to their masters, he begins by making it the *general* duty of all Christians to each other (which includes husbands, parents and masters). Humble submission is such an important part of Christian behaviour that the verb occurs thirty-two times in the New Testament. Not self-assertion but self-submission is the hall-mark of the Spirit-filled Christian.

Sometimes, it is true, when a fundamental theological or moral principle is at stake, we must not give way. Paul gave an outstanding example of this need for firmness when he opposed Peter in a direct and public confrontation at Antioch (Gal. 2:11–14). But we must always beware lest our supposed stand on principle is in reality an ugly exhibition of pride. It is wise to distrust our righteous indignation; in it there is usually more than a smattering of unrighteous vanity. The test is in the last words of the sentence: 'out of reverence for Christ.' Our first duty is reverent and humble submission to the Lord Christ. We should submit to others right up to the point where our submission to them would mean disloyalty to Christ.

The wholesome results of the fullness of the Spirit are now laid bare. The two chief spheres in which this fullness is manifest are worship and fellowship. If we are filled with the Spirit, we shall be praising Christ and thanking our Father, and we shall be speaking and submitting to one another. The Holy Spirit puts us in a right relationship with both God and man. It is in these spiritual qualities and activities, not in supernatural phenomena, that we should look for primary evidence of the Holy Spirit's fullness. This is the apostle's emphasis when he is dealing with the subject in his Corinthian and Ephesian letters, as also when he outlines 'the fruit of the Spirit' in his letter to the Galatians (see the next chapter).

The command to be filled

We now come back to the command, upon which depend the four present participles which we have been considering. This command is: 'be filled with the Spirit.' Notice these four points about the verb.

First, it is in the *imperative* mood. 'Be filled' is not a tentative suggestion, a mild recommendation, a polite piece of advice. It is a command which comes to us from Christ with all the authority of one of his chosen apostles. We have no more liberty to escape this duty than we have the ethical duties which surround the text, *e.g.* to speak the truth, to do honest work, to be kind and forgiving to one another, or to live lives of purity and love. The fullness of the Holy Spirit is not optional for the Christian, but obligatory.

Secondly, the verb is in the *plural* form. So is the preceding verb 'do not get drunk with wine'. Both imperatives in Ephesians 5:18, the prohibition and the command, are written to the whole Christian community. They are universal in their application. We are none of us to get drunk; we are all of us to be Spirit-filled. The fullness of the Holy Spirit is emphatically not a privilege reserved for some, but a duty resting upon all. Like the command to sobriety and self-control, the command to seek the Spirit's fullness is addressed without exception to all the people of God.

Thirdly, the verb is in the *passive* voice: 'be filled'. That is, 'let the Holy Spirit fill you' (NEB). An important condition of enjoying his fullness is to yield to him without reserve. Nevertheless, it must not be imagined that we are purely passive agents in receiving the Spirit's fullness, any more than in getting drunk. A man gets drunk by drinking; we become filled with the Spirit by drinking too, as we have already seen from our Lord's teaching in John 7:37.

Fourthly, the verb is in the *present* tense. It is well known that, in the Greek language, if the imperative is aorist it refers to a single action, while if it is present the action is continuous. Thus, when at the wedding in Cana Jesus said, 'fill the jars with water' (Jn. 2:7), the aorist imperative shows that he meant them to do it once only. The present imperative 'be filled with the Spirit', on the other hand, indicates not some dramatic or decisive experience which will settle the issue for good, but a continuous appropriation.

This is further enforced in the letter to the Ephesians by the contrast between the 'sealing' and the 'filling' of the Spirit. Twice the apostle writes that his readers have been 'sealed' with the Holy Spirit (Eph. 1:13; 4:30). The aorists are identical and describe every penitent believer. God has accepted him and placed upon him the seal of the Spirit, to authenticate him, to mark and to secure him as his own. But although all believers are 'sealed', not all believers remain 'filled', for the sealing is past and finished, while the filling is (or should be) present and continuous.

Perhaps an illustration will help at this point to show that the fullness of the Spirit is intended to be not a static but a developing experience. Let us compare two people. One is a baby, new-born and weighing 7 pounds, who has just begun to breathe; the other is a full-grown man, 6 feet in height and 12 stone in weight. Both are fit and healthy; both are breathing properly; and both may be described as 'filled with air'. What, then, is the difference between them? It lies in the capacity of their lungs. Both are 'filled', yet one is more filled than the other because his capacity is so much greater.

The same is true of spiritual life and growth. Who will deny that a new-born babe in Christ is filled with the Spirit?

The body of every believer is the temple of the Holy Spirit (1 Cor. 6:19); are we to suppose that, when the Spirit enters his temple, he does not fill it? A mature and godly Christian of many years' standing is filled with the Spirit also. The difference between them is to be found in what might be called their spiritual lung-capacity, namely the measure of their believing grasp of God's purpose for them.

This is clear from the apostle's first prayer for the Ephesian Christians. He prays:

'that the God of our Lord Jesus Christ, the Father of glory, may give you a spirit (or, perhaps, 'Spirit') of wisdom and of revelation in the knowledge of him, having the eyes of your hearts enlightened, that you may know what is the hope to which he has called you, what are the riches of his glorious inheritance in the saints, and what is the immeasurable greatness of his power in us who believe...' (1:17–19).

This passage unfolds the stages of spiritual progress. It is those who 'believe' who experience the fullness of God's power. But first they must 'know' its greatness, and for this they need the enlightenment of their heart's eyes by the Holy Spirit.

This, then, is the order: enlightenment, knowledge, faith, experience. It is by enlightenment that we know, and by faith that we enter into the enjoyment of what we know. Our faith-experience is therefore largely conditioned by our heart-knowledge. Further, the more we know, the greater our spiritual capacity becomes and the greater our responsibility to claim our inheritance by faith. Thus, when a person is newly born of the Spirit, his grasp of God's purpose for him is usually very limited and his experience is limited in proportion. But as the Holy Spirit enlightens the eyes of his heart, vistas begin to open up before him of which at first he had scarcely even dreamed. He begins to see and know the hope of God's calling, the riches of God's inheritance and the greatness of God's power. He is challenged to embrace by faith the fullness of God's purpose for him. The tragedy is that often our faith does not keep pace with our knowledge. Our eyes are opened to see more and more of the wonders of God's purpose for us in Christ, but we hang back from appropriating it by faith. This is one of the ways in which we lose the fullness of the Spirit, not necessarily by disobedience but by disbelief. Our lungs develop, but we do not use them. We need constantly to repent of our unbelief and to cry to God to increase our faith, so that, as our knowledge grows, our faith may grow with it and we may continuously lay hold of more of the greatness of God's purpose and power.

The average Christian

So far in this chapter we have sought to distinguish between the baptism of the Spirit (received once for all at conversion) and the fullness of the Spirit (to be continuously and increasingly appropriated). We have also taken a look at some important teaching of our Lord and of his apostle Paul on the need to keep coming and drinking, the marks of the Spirit's fullness and the command to be filled. All this has been a biblical study.

But the chief objections to this interpretation are not biblical so much as empirical, not theoretical but practical. Let me state them in two sentences:

a. If all Christians have been baptized with the Spirit, the majority do not appear to have been!

b. Some Christians claim to have received a further and distinct experience of the Holy Spirit, and *their* claim does appear to be true!

We shall examine both objections in turn.

First we take what may be called the 'average Christian'

today. 'Can it be seriously maintained', we are asked, 'that he has been baptized with the Spirit? Look at his conversion and at his subsequent life. His conversion was quite unspectacular and not at all like a "baptism of the Spirit", while his present Christian living supplies little or no evidence of his having been thus baptized.' What are we to say in reply?

The denial that Christian conversion today is or includes a baptism with the Spirit depends on an *a priori* assumption regarding what the baptism of the Spirit must invariably be like. All the time people have at the back of their minds the dramatic events of the Day of Pentecost. They are looking for wind and fire and foreign languages. They forget that the supernatural signs which accompanied the coming of the Spirit at Pentecost are no more typical of every baptism of the Spirit than the supernatural signs which accompanied the conversion of Saul on the Damascus road are typical of every Christian conversion. We have already seen that the gift of 'languages' or 'tongues' cannot possibly be made an indispensable evidence of the baptism of the Spirit. The same is true of the wind and fire. No wind, fire or languages are mentioned at the end of Acts 2 in relation to the 3,000 who received the Spirit. No. The wind, the fire and the languages at Pentecost, like the light and the voice on the Damascus road, were the dramatic outward accompaniments; they were no necessary part of the essential inward experience. What biblical warrant is there for supposing that people cannot receive the 'gift' or 'baptism' of the Spirit in a quiet and unsensational way?

I would go further. There is no biblical warrant for the view that regeneration is a conscious process, that is to say, that the person being born again is conscious of what is happening inside him. Jesus himself indicated the opposite when in his conversation with Nicodemus he drew an analogy between the Spirit's work in the new birth and the blowing of the wind:

64

'The wind blows where it wills, and you hear the sound of it, but you do not know whence it comes or whither it goes; so it is with every one who is born of the Spirit' (Jn. 3:8).

Although the effects of the wind are seen, heard and felt, there is something secret and mysterious about the operation of the wind itself. The effects of the new birth are evident too (in a changed life), but there is something secret and mysterious about the regenerating work of the Holy Spirit. Of course, 'conversion' (the sinner's turning to Christ in repentance and faith), which is also a work of the Spirit, is normally conscious, as he grasps certain things with his mind and acts with his will. But regeneration is the implantation of new life into a soul dead in trespasses and sins. We are no more conscious of this infusion of spiritual life, called rebirth or spiritual birth, than we are of our physical birth. In both cases self-consciousness, consciousness of being alive, develops later. Therefore, if 'baptism with the Spirit' is, as we have argued, another way of referring to birth of the Spirit, there is no reason to insist that it must be conscious, let alone dramatic.

The other part of the objection regarding the 'average' Christian concerns not the circumstances of his conversion but the low level of his subsequent Christian living. Can it be held that such a person has been baptized with the Spirit? Well, I certainly have no wish to deny or excuse the sub-normality of much of our Christian living today. It is often true, and whenever it is true it is sad. Our disobedience and our unbelief have robbed many of us of our full inheritance. It is still ours by right, because we are Christ's, but we have failed to enter into it. We are like the Israelites when they had been given the promised land but had not yet taken possession of it. We need to repent and to return to God. We have indeed been baptized with the Spirit, but we continue to live on a level lower than our Spirit-baptism has made possible, because we do not remain filled with the Spirit.

It has to be added that, alas, this low level of Christian living is to be found in all groups of Christians. Both those who claim exciting spiritual experiences and those who do not can fail in moral duties, in honesty, purity and unselfishness. Equally I have known some in both groups who are beautifully Christlike. The failure and poor performance of many Christians are evidence *not of their need to be baptized with the Spirit* (even the proud, loveless, quarrelsome and sin-tolerant Corinthian Christians had been baptized with the Spirit), *but of their need to recover the fullness of the Spirit* which they have lost through sin or unbelief, thus becoming what the Corinthian Christians were, namely 'unspiritual' or 'carnal' (1 Cor. 3:1 ff.). In this sense many Christians do have an experience in two stages or more. But this is not the general will and purpose of God (which is a continuous and increasing appropriation); it is due rather to their sinful backsliding.

Special experiences

I turn to the second category of Christians mentioned above, not the average Christian who (it is said) does not appear to have been baptized with the Spirit, but those particular Christians who (it is claimed) have had a 'pentecostal' experience which they call a 'baptism with the Spirit'. What are we to say about them and their experiences?

I mention in passing three explanations which we should not forget, but on which I will not spend time. First, a small number of such experiences are no doubt *demonic*, a horrible satanic counterfeit of genuine spiritual experience. Jesus warned us of such things, and the alarming contemporary spread of fascination with the occult should put us on our guard. Spurious satanic deceptions should not deceive God's children, however. The devil hates both Christ and holiness, and we shall not find Christ honoured or holiness promoted where he is in control.

Secondly, a larger number are *psychological*. Of course in a sense all our experiences are psychological. But what I mean is that some experiences which we think are spiritual are in reality psychological, because they originate in our human psyche rather than in the Spirit of God. This is certainly true of some so-called 'tongue-speaking'. Of how much I am not qualified to say. But some kind of 'glosso-lalia', of involuntary speech beyond the control of the conscious mind, is well known in Hindu, Muslim and Mormon circles, as well as in some medical conditions, and this phenomenon does not appear to be different from what many Christians claim today. This need not cause us too much anxiety, however. To attribute something to the human psyche is not the same as to attribute it to the devil. What is 'psychological' may be morally and spiritually neutral. It is much more important to ask whether it glorifies Christ and promotes righteousness.

Thirdly, some other contemporary experiences appear to be in reality *conversion* experiences. When one hears of nominal, liberal or Catholic Christians claiming to be 'baptized with the Spirit', one often suspects that they are really describing what used to be called an 'evangelical experience', that is, their conversion, in which case their description of what has happened to them is more biblical than they may realize!

Having mentioned these three explanations, I am concerned now to look at experiences which appear to be neither demonic nor purely psychological, and which also are evidently not conversion experiences, because they happen to Christians who have been converted for many years. On the contrary, they are authentic, deeper experiences of God. About these, undoubtedly the first thing to be said is that the Holy Spirit is God the Lord. He is the divine Spirit, the mighty Spirit, the free and sovereign Spirit. We should have no wish to attempt to limit his working; indeed, even if we wished to, we could not. Although I believe we must insist that, according to the New Testament, God's *norm* is one initiatory 'baptism' with the Spirit, followed by a continuous and increasing appropriation of his fullness which involves a steady growth in holiness and into Christian maturity, yet it must be added that within this process of growth there may be many deeper experiences and that sometimes the Spirit works more abnormally still. In writing about these further experiences, I would emphasize first their varied character, next their secondary importance and thirdly their continuing incompleteness.

First, their *variety*. Under the heading of this word I include the fact that the same or similar experiences may be repeated. We have already noted that the New Testament teaching may be summed up as 'one baptism, many fillings'. A fresh filling may precede a fresh responsibility and be given to equip us for new and exacting work. Or it may follow a period of disobedience, declension or dryness, and the penitent believer may find himself suddenly lifted to a new plane of spiritual awareness and reality.

To some extent these experiences will vary according to our natural temperament. The Holy Spirit respects us as human beings and does not obliterate by new creation what we already are by creation. He works within us in ways appropriate to ourselves, setting us free to be ourselves according to the full potential of our created being. But our basic temperament remains unchanged, which is one major reason for the wide variety of spiritual experiences. One would not, and should not, expect so-called 'phlegmatic' and 'choleric' types, or extroverts and introverts, to experience Christ in identical terms.

Yet *all* Christians can expect fresh experiences of God. God is no lover of staleness or stagnation. He bids us sing a *new* song, because he means our knowledge of him to be new, and he promises that his mercies will be 'new every morning'

(Ps. 40:3; 98:1; La. 3:23). Sometimes the Holy Spirit's inward witness, assuring us that we are indeed God's children, is strongly and wonderfully confirmed so that we are completely delivered from darkness and doubt. Sometimes he floods our hearts with such a tidal wave of his love that we almost ask him to stay his hand lest we be drowned by it. Sometimes our hearts 'burn within us' as Christ opens to us the Scriptures and we see him in the Scriptures as we have never seen him before (Lk. 24: 27, 32). Sometimes we experience a quickening of our spiritual pulse, a leaping of our heart, a kindling of our love for God and man, a pervading sense of peace and well-being. Sometimes in the dignified reverence of public worship, or in the spontaneous fellowship of a home meeting, or at the Lord's Table, or in private prayer, invisible reality overwhelms us. Time stands still. We step into a new dimension of eternity. We become still and *know* that God is God. We fall down before him and worship.

Already in trying to describe the indescribable we have seen that each member of the Trinity is involved. Christian experience is experience of God: Father, Son and Holy Spirit. There really is no such thing as 'an experience of the Holy Spirit' from which the Father and the Son are excluded. In any case, the Holy Spirit is a reticent Spirit. He does not willingly draw attention to himself. Rather he prompts us to pray 'Abba! Father!' and thus witnesses to our filial relationship to God (Rom. 8:15, 16; Gal. 4:6). And above all he glorifies Christ. He turns the bright beams of his searchlight upon the face of Jesus Christ. He is never more satisfied than when the believer is engrossed in Jesus Christ. It was in the context of the Spirit's coming that Jesus said:

'He who has my commandments and keeps them, he it is who loves me; and he who loves me will be loved by my Father, and I will love him and manifest myself to him' (Jn. 14:21).

The true lover of Jesus, who proves his love by his obedience, can conceive no greater reward than this promised manifestation of his Beloved by the Spirit. It brings what Peter called 'unutterable and exalted joy' (1 Pet. 1:8).

These deeper experiences which I have so far mentioned might be called 'usual', because they relate to the assurance, love, joy and peace which Scripture indicates are common to all believers, in some measure. It would surprise me if any Christian reader is a complete stranger to them all. But there are other experiences, to which I must now come, of a more 'unusual' kind because they are not part of the regular Christian experience which the New Testament portrays. Sometimes the Holy Spirit may even give to the believer what he gave to the apostle Paul, 'visions and revelations of the Lord', so that Paul said he was 'caught up to the third heaven' and 'heard things that cannot be told, which man may not utter' (2 Cor. 12:1–4). Sometimes, especially in times of revival, believers have claimed quite extraordinary experiences and visitations of God. Sometimes a Christian evangelist or preacher is given a marvellous access of supernatural power for the particular ministry to which God has called him. We have probably read of such experiences in the biographies of great men of God such as John Wesley and George Whitefield, of Jonathan Edwards and David Brainerd, of D. L. Moody and others. In biblical terms we might say that such men were 'anointed' with the Holy Spirit. We should use the word cautiously, because in one sense all Christians have been 'anointed' with, or have received the 'anointing' of, the Holy Spirit (2 Cor. 1:21, AV; 1 Jn. 2:20, 27). Nevertheless, Scripture also uses this language for special situations, as when Jesus applied Isaiah 61:1 to himself at the beginning of his public ministry and claimed 'the Spirit of the Lord is upon me, because he has anointed me to preach . . .' (Lk. 4:18). Perhaps this is also how we should understand what happened to Saul of Tarsus when Ananias visited him. He was to be 'filled with the Holy Spirit' (Acts 9:17) in order to be 'a witness' for Christ to all men of what he had seen and heard (22:14; *cf.* 26:16–18). It was his commissioning and anointing as an apostle.

It is the great variety of such experiences which we need at this stage to observe. I have no wish to doubt or question their validity. What worries me is the wooden stereotype which a few zealous souls try to impose on everybody, when they insist on a so-called 'baptism of the Spirit' subsequent to conversion, which must take a certain shape and be accompanied, or followed, by certain signs. It is this that I feel obliged to reject as incompatible with Scripture. But let us not replace one stereotype by another! All we can say is that the Christian life begins with a new birth, which may take place in a variety of different ways but includes the 'gift' or 'baptism' of the Spirit, and that it is followed by growth into maturity, a process which may include a wide diversity of deeper experiences.

From the varied character of these experiences I turn to a consideration of their *secondary importance*. They may be deeply moving, even exciting. But none of them can possibly compare in importance with God's first work of grace when he had mercy on us and reconciled us to himself. Some Christians talk of their further experiences in exaggerated language, as if previously they were in bondage, now they are free, formerly everything was watery, now the water has turned into wine. But they must be mistaking subjective feelings for objective reality. For when we become united to Christ by faith, something so tremendous happens that the New Testament cannot find language adequate to describe it. It is a new birth, yes, but also a new creation, a resurrection, light out of darkness, and life from the dead. We were slaves, now we are sons. We were lost, now we have come home. We were condemned and under the wrath of God, now we have been justified and adopted into his family. What subsequent experience can possibly compare with this in importance? We must be careful, in describing deeper experiences, not to denigrate regeneration or to cast a slur on this first, decisive and creative work of God's love.

My third point about subsequent experiences is that they are all *incomplete*. Some speak of theirs in such a way as to suggest not only that nothing much had happened to them before, but that nothing much more could happen to them after! They give the impression that they have arrived. This was the Corinthian self-satisfaction which Paul described with such biting sarcasm:

> 'Already you are filled! Already you have become rich! Without us you have become kings! And would that you did reign, so that we might share the rule with you!' (1 Cor. 4:8).

They behaved as if they were enjoying their own little private millennium! But the same New Testament which speaks in such strong terms of what God has done for us in Christ keeps reminding us that we have only begun to enter into our inheritance. We are to hunger and thirst for more in this life, and to know that only in the next shall we hunger no more, neither thirst any more. Thus in the New Testament we find side by side expressions of affirmation and of aspiration, of satisfaction and of dissatisfaction. On the one hand 'we rejoice', on the other 'we groan' (*e.g.* Rom. 8:23; 2 Cor. 5:2). It is true that joy is part of the fruit of the Spirit, but there is also such a thing as Christian sorrow. Some Christians speak and look as if they thought they should wear on their face a perpetual grin! By contrast, we read of the Old Testament saint whose 'eyes shed streams of tears' because men were disobeying God's law (Ps. 119:136), of the Lord Jesus himself who wept over the impenitent city of Jerusalem (Lk. 19:41), and of his apostle Paul who on occasions could write only 'with tears' (*e.g.* Phil. 3:18). I sometimes wish we could see more Christian tears today, and I wish more of us were sensitive Christians, deeply disturbed by, and weeping for, the continuing sin-fulness of the world, the church and our own heart. Not till the consummation will God wipe away all tears from our eyes (Rev. 21:4).

An exhortation

To conclude this section, I take the liberty of issuing a per-sonal and practical exhortation – first to those of us who do not claim to have received any exceptional mani-festations of the Holy Spirit; secondly to those who do; and thirdly to all of us, whatever our experiences may have been.

First, let me address those who, though we have had perhaps many deeper experiences of the more 'usual' type, may have received no unusual experiences of the Holy Spirit. It would be easy for us, through fear or pride or envy, to question or even deny the validity of such experi-ences when claimed by others. But it would be wrong for us to do so for no better reason than that others claim to have had them, while we have not. We must certainly 'test everything' and in particular 'test the spirits' (1 Thes. 5:21; 1 Jn. 4:1). We may also feel it wise in regard to some claims to suspend judgment. At the same time, provided that there is nothing in the claimed experience which is contrary to Scripture, and provided that the fruits of the experience seem to be beneficial to the believer and edifying to the church, we must be humbly ready to recognize the unusual operations of the Holy Spirit in others and at least say with Gamaliel: 'Let them alone; for if this plan or this under-taking is of men, it will fail; but if it is of God, you will not be able to overthrow them. You might even be found opposing God!' (Acts 5:38, 39). We all need, in these days in which the Holy Spirit seems to be stirring, to be sensitive to what he may be saying and doing among us. We must be very careful neither to blaspheme against the Holy Spirit by attributing his work to the devil, nor to quench the Holy

Spirit by resolving to contain him within our own safe, traditional patterns. On the other hand, we should also not manifest a sinful discontent with his more normal and usual operations in us. Abnormal experiences are not necessary to Christian maturity. We should rejoice in what we do know of the Holy Spirit as teacher and witness, and in the love, joy, peace and power which he has given us.

Secondly, a word to those who may have been given some unusual visitation of the Spirit. You are, of course, thanking God for the great grace he has granted to you; but remember that the Holy Spirit is a sovereign Spirit. He not only distributes different spiritual gifts 'as he wills' (1 Cor. 12:11), but he exercises his unusual ministries according to his will also. It is understandable that you should want to bear witness to what God has done for you. But I beg you not to seek to stereotype everybody's spiritual experience, or even to imagine that the Holy Spirit necessarily purposes to give to others what he has given to you. It is spiritual *graces* which should be common to all Christians, not spiritual *gifts* or spiritual *experiences*. In a word, let your experience lead you to worship and praise; but let your exhortation to others be grounded not upon your experiences but upon Scripture. More particularly, I would appeal to you not to urge upon people a 'baptism with the Spirit' as a second and subsequent experience entirely distinct from conversion, for this cannot be proved from Scripture. Instead, please urge upon us what *is* constantly urged in Scripture, namely that we should not grieve or quench the Holy Spirit (Eph. 4:30; 1 Thes. 5:19), but rather walk in the Spirit, and be filled with the Spirit (Gal. 5:16; Eph. 5:18). Urge these things upon us, and we shall be thankful.

Thirdly, an exhortation to us all, whatever our spiritual condition may be. Let us constantly seek to be filled with the Spirit, to be led by the Spirit, to walk in the Spirit. Can we not gladly occupy this common ground together, so that there is no division among us? Further, we can agree that the main condition of being filled is to be hungry. The Scripture tells us that God fills the hungry with good things and sends the rich empty away. 'Open your mouth wide,' he says, 'and I will fill it' (Ps. 81:10). This does not mean that we can ever in this life be filled to hunger no more. Of course, God in Christ through the Spirit does satisfy our hunger and quench our thirst, but it is only of the next life that it is finally written 'they shall hunger no more, neither thirst any more' (Rev. 7:16). In this life our hunger is satisfied only to break out again. Jesus said, 'Blessed are those who hunger and thirst for righteousness' (Mt. 5:6), implying that hungering and thirsting after righteousness is as much a permanent state of the Christian as being 'poor in spirit' or 'meek' or 'merciful'. So let neither those who have had unusual experiences, nor those who have not, imagine that they have 'attained', and that God cannot fill them any fuller with himself! We all need to hear and obey the gracious invitation of Jesus: 'If any one thirst, let him come to me and drink.' We must learn to keep coming to Jesus and to keep drinking. Only so, in the wise and balanced language of the Book of Common Prayer, shall we 'daily increase in the Holy Spirit more and more, until we come unto God's everlasting kingdom'.

3 The Fruit of the Spirit

I have already referred more than once to 'the fruit of the Spirit'. It is time now to examine in greater detail what is meant by this. The expression comes from Paul's letter to the Galatians. These are his words:

'But the fruit of the Spirit is love, joy, peace, patience, kindness, goodness, faithfulness, gentleness, self-control' (Gal. 5:22, 23a).

The mere recital of these Christian graces should be enough to make the mouth water and the heart beat faster. For this is a portrait of Jesus Christ. No man or woman has ever exhibited these qualities in such balance or to such perfection as the man Christ Jesus. Yet this is the kind of person that every Christian longs to be.

Various attempts have been made to classify the nine qualities Paul lists. No classification is altogether satisfactory, however, and there is a danger of imposing an artificial one. Perhaps the simplest is to take them as three triads, which depict our Christian relationship first to God, next to others and lastly to ourselves.

First our relationship with God: 'love, joy, peace'. The Holy Spirit puts God's love in our hearts, God's joy in our souls and God's peace in our minds. Love, joy and peace pervade a Spirit-filled Christian. Indeed, these may be said to be his principal and abiding characteristics. Everything he does is conceived in love, undertaken with joy and accomplished in peace.

Secondly, our relationship with others: 'patience, kindness, goodness'. Here is the patience which bears rudeness and unkindness from others and refuses to retaliate; the kindness which goes beyond the negative toleration of not wishing anybody any harm to the positive benevolence of wishing everybody well; and the goodness which turns wish into deed, and takes the initiative to serve people in concrete, constructive ways. It is not difficult to see 'patience kindness, goodness' as three ascending steps in our attitude to others.

Thirdly, our relationship with ourselves: 'faithfulness, gentleness, self-control'. The word for 'faithfulness' is that usually translated 'faith' (*pistis*). But here it seems to mean not the faith which relies on Christ or on others, but the faithfulness which invites others to rely on us. More simply, it is not trust but trustworthiness, the solid dependability of those who always keep their promises and finish their tasks. Gentleness is a quality not of the soft and weak, but of the strong and energetic, whose strength and energy are kept under control. Self-control is mastery of our tongue, thoughts, appetites and passions.

This, then, is the portrait of Christ, and so – at least in the ideal – of the balanced, Christlike, Spirit-filled Christian. We have no liberty to pick and choose among these qualities. For it is together (as a bunch of fruit or a harvest) that they constitute Christlikeness; to cultivate some without the others is to be a lop-sided Christian. The Spirit gives different Christians different gifts, as we shall consider further in the next chapter, but he works to produce the same fruit in all. He is not content if we display love for others, while we have no control of ourselves; or interior joy and peace without kindness to others; or a negative patience without a positive goodness; or gentleness and pliability without the firmness of Christian dependability. The lop-sided Christian is a carnal Christian; but there is a whole-ness, a roundness, a fullness of Christian character which only the Spirit-filled Christian ever exhibits.

But how can these qualities be developed? That is the question we want to address to the apostle. His answer comes back to us from the fact that all nine qualities are gathered together under the single expression 'the fruit of the Spirit'. Important truths emerge from this metaphor.

Supernatural origin

The first truth is that the fruit of the Spirit is supernatural in its origin. This is evident, because the qualities he lists are the fruit of *the Spirit*. The Holy Spirit himself is credited with their production. They are the harvest which he grows and gathers in the lives of the people he fills.

It is further evident from the context, for 'the fruit of the Spirit' is deliberately contrasted with 'the works of the flesh'. 'The flesh' in Pauline language does not normally refer to the substance which covers our bony skeleton, but denotes ourselves, our whole selves as we are by nature, fallen, sinful and selfish. 'The Spirit', on the other hand, refers not to another part of us, our spirit, but to the Holy Spirit of God himself who dwells in Christian people and is concerned to transform them into the image of Christ. In the light of this distinction between 'flesh' and 'Spirit', we may say that 'the works of the flesh' are deeds we do *naturally* when left to our own resources, while 'the fruit of the Spirit' consists of qualities which the Spirit works in us *supernaturally* (for they are beyond our natural strength) when we are responding to him.

If we are left to ourselves, what appears naturally is such sins as 'immorality, impurity, licentiousness . . . drunken-ness, carousing' (verses 19, 21), whereas the supernatural fruit of the Spirit is the opposite, such virtues as 'reliability, gentleness, self-control'. Left to ourselves, we rebel against God and lapse into 'idolatry and sorcery' (verse 20), but the Holy Spirit leads us into 'love, joy, peace'. Again, the works of the flesh are such antisocial blemishes as 'enmity, strife, jealousy, anger, selfishness, dissension, party spirit, envy' (verses 20, 21), whereas the corresponding fruit of the Spirit is 'patience, kindness, goodness'.

It is clear, then, that by nature all our relationships are awry. We turn away from God to idols. We fall out with other people and live in discord. We indulge ourselves instead of controlling ourselves. To live in harmony with God and others, and in firm control of ourselves, this is a supernatural work of God's grace. It is 'the fruit of the Spirit'.

Indeed, this fruit (the sum total of these Christian qualities) is the best available evidence – because it is solidly objective – of the indwelling fullness of the Holy Spirit. The real proof of a deep work of the Spirit of God in any human being is neither subjective, emotional experiences, nor spectacular signs, but moral, Christlike qualities. Here is a Christian who makes great claims in the realm of experience, but lacks love, joy, peace, kindness and self-control: I think all of us will say that there is something wrong with his claims. But here is another Christian who, whatever his experiences and gifts may be, brings us in his character a sweet savour of the Lord Jesus: it is surely his company that we all prefer. For we see in him a token of God's grace and a temple of the Holy Spirit.

Natural growth

The next truth we have to notice is that these qualities are described as the Spirit's *fruit*. And, given the right conditions, all fruit grows naturally. True, we sometimes talk of 'forcing' plants by putting them under glass in a greenhouse at a certain temperature. But all we mean by 'force' in this context is that we accelerate their growth by providing artificially the conditions in which they grow naturally. For the process of growth itself (even in a greenhouse) is not artificial; it is still natural.

By calling Christian character 'the fruit of the Spirit' the apostle Paul was teaching that it is both supernatural in origin (being *the Spirit's* fruit) and natural in growth (being the Spirit's *fruit*). It is important to hold these two truths in balance, not least for the following reason. The fact that holy living is a product of the Holy Spirit might easily lead people to suppose that they have nothing to contribute to the process themselves. But the fact that the Spirit produces it as his 'fruit' indicates at once that there are certain conditions on which the growth depends and for which we have to take responsibility. For what is natural is always conditional. It becomes a natural process only when the conditions are right.

This lesson from horticulture applies equally to growth into Christian maturity. Paul himself makes the application, although not in Galatians 5 but in Galatians 6. Here is a good example of the need to see each text in a broad context and to disregard the arbitrary chapter divisions of our English Bibles. For if in chapter 5 he writes about 'fruit', in chapter 6 he comes to the question of 'sowing' on which all harvesting of fruit ultimately depends. These are his words:

'Do not be deceived; God is not mocked, for whatever a man sows, that he will also reap. For he who sows to his own flesh will from the flesh reap corruption; but he who sows to the Spirit will from the Spirit reap eternal life' (6: 7, 8).

The fundamental principle is stated in the epigram 'whatever a man sows, that he will also reap'. It is an inflexible principle of all God's dealings, a law of his own consistency, in both the physical and the moral realms, in both nature and human character. Always, invariably, we reap what we sow. Therefore, because of this faithfulness of God, we can determine in advance what we shall reap by deciding what we shall sow. If I were a farmer wanting to harvest a crop of oats, I would have to sow oats. It would be ludicrous to sow barley or wheat instead. The same principle applies to human behaviour. If the Holy Spirit is to produce good fruit in our lives, then we have to sow good seed. The old proverb puts it well:

> Sow a thought, and you reap an act;
> Sow an act, and you reap a habit;
> Sow a habit, and you reap a character;
> Sow a character, and you reap a destiny.

We cannot alter this. As Paul put it, 'God is not mocked'. The Greek verb he chose is very graphic. It means literally 'to turn one's nose up at' someone. He meant that we cannot treat God with contempt or despise the laws he has laid down. Yet some Christians are surprised that they are not reaping the fruit of the Spirit, although they spend a great deal of their time sowing to the flesh. Do they suppose that they can cheat or fool God, and bend his laws to their convenience?

Consider more precisely what the apostle means. He likens our personality to a field in which every day we are sowing. It is a divided field. One section he calls 'the flesh' (ourselves or what we are by nature), and the other section 'the Spirit' (the Holy Spirit or what we are by grace). It is possible to sow in either section of the field. One Christian 'sows to his own flesh', while another 'sows to the Spirit'. As a result, each reaps a different harvest. What is this sowing? And what is this harvest?

By the 'sowing' the apostle appears to be referring to the whole pattern of our thoughts and habits, our life-style, life-direction and life-discipline. It includes the company we keep, the friendships we cultivate, the literature we read, the films we watch in the cinema or on television, the kind of pursuits with which we occupy our leisure, and everything which engrosses our interest, absorbs our energy and dominates our mind. About all these things we have to make a decision, regarding both the general trend of our life and the myriad lesser choices which present themselves to us each day. For by these things we are sowing, sowing, sowing all the time; and according to what and where we sow, thus shall we reap. Again and again Paul reverts to this theme in his letters, and illustrates it with an abundance of metaphor. Now it is our clothing (what we take off and what we put on). Now it is a question of athletic prowess (running away from some things and running fast after others.) Now it is a matter of life and death (actually killing, even by crucifixion, our sinful desires and passions, and instead living sensitively to the Spirit's promptings). Now it is the business of paying our debts (for we are debtors to the Spirit, not the flesh). Of all these images, however, none emphasizes the *naturalness* of Christian growth in holiness more, granted the right conditions, than the need to sow the right seed in the right field if we hope to reap the right harvest.

What harvest? To sow to the flesh, he says, is to reap 'corruption'. It is an ugly word, conjuring up horrific images of decay, decomposition, death and rotting corpses. It probably signifies not only a steadily deteriorating character in this life, but also ruin in the next. To sow to the Spirit, by contrast, is to reap 'eternal life', namely a deepening fellowship with the living God now (to know whom is eternal life, Jn. 17:3), together with that fullness of fellowship with him which defies imagination and which awaits us on the last day. Thus not only our moral character in this world, but also our ultimate destiny in the next, depends on what seed we are sowing now, and where we are sowing it.

Gradual maturity
There is a third lesson to learn from the apostle's use of this 'fruit' metaphor. Even a very elementary knowledge of botany is sufficient for us to be aware that God's processes

ripen slowly. As Jesus put it in one of his parables about corn: 'first the blade, then the ear, then the full grain in the ear.' Or, as we might say of fruit-growing – first the leaf; then the flower bud; then the blossom; then the fertilized fruit as a kind of embryo, but still hard, green and uninviting; then the swelling, the softening and the first blush of colour; and finally the ripe, juicy fruit in the summer. It is a process which is natural, conditional and gradual. What is true of the fruit of the orchard is equally true of the fruit of the Spirit. The Holy Spirit implants life in the soul instantaneously at the new birth (however many months of preparation may have preceded it); but he takes time, a long time, to produce a ripe Christian character.

This emphasis on the gradualness of sanctification is not meant to condone our continued sinfulness, or to encourage our laziness, or to lower our expectations, but rather to warn us against quack gardeners who offer us ripe fruit on the spot. For ours is more the age of machinery than of agriculture. Its symbol is rather the hammer than the sickle. Automation implies speed. The computer gives you answers within seconds. But the Holy Spirit is not in a hurry. Character is the produce of a lifetime.

Understanding the gradualness of God's work should make us more active in our collaboration with the Spirit (the heavenly gardener) in his fruit-growing, more watchful over our sowing if we care about reaping a good crop, and more disciplined in our habits of public and private devotion, so that by these God-given means of grace we may grow in grace, and the fruit of the Spirit may swell and ripen in us.

Charles Simeon, Cambridge don and vicar at the beginning of the last century, whose profound influence under God is still felt today, was nevertheless by nature and disposition a hot-tempered, proud and impetuous man. When he paid his first visit to his fellow-evangelical Henry Venn at Yelling, the latter's eldest daughter vividly described it.

The incident is recorded by Michael Hennell: ' "It is impossible to conceive anything more ridiculous than his look and manner were. His grimaces were beyond anything you can imagine. So, as soon as he were gone, we all got together into the study, and set up an amazing laugh." But their father summoned them into the garden and, though it was early summer, asked them to pick him one of the green peaches. When they showed surprise, he said: "Well, my dears, it is green now, and we must wait; but a little more sun, and a few more showers, and the peach will be ripe and sweet. So it is with Mr Simeon." '[1] And so it proved to be, for as he sowed he reaped, and under the gracious influence of the Holy Spirit he became a gentle, humble, loving, Christlike character.

Application

I began by listing and classifying the nine Christian qualities which together make up 'the fruit of the Spirit' and suggested that the mere rehearsal of these qualities should be enough to whet the Christian's spiritual appetite. Indeed, I take it for granted that we 'hunger and thirst for righteousness' and 'seek first God's kingdom and his righteousness' (Mt. 5:6; 6:33). We have also considered three reasons why these qualities are termed the Spirit's fruit. In conclusion, we could learn a lesson from each.

First, since Christlikeness is supernatural in its origin, we need both *humility* and *faith* – the humility to acknowledge that *we* cannot produce this harvest by ourselves, out of the soil of 'the flesh', and the faith to believe that *God* can cause it to ripen within us as the fruit of the Spirit. Thus Jesus taught: 'Abide in me, and I in you. As the branch cannot bear fruit by itself, unless it abides in the vine, neither can you, unless you abide in me' (Jn. 15:4). Holiness begins with self-despair, for it is only out of self-despair

[1] Michael Hennell, *John Venn and the Clapham Sect* (Lutterworth Press, London, 1958), pp. 89, 90.

that faith is born. To put no confidence in the flesh, because of our conviction that in it 'nothing good dwells' (Rom. 7:18), is an essential preliminary to full confidence in the Spirit.

Secondly, since Christlikeness is natural in its growth, granted the right conditions, we need *discipline* to ensure that the conditions are right. Only what is sown can be reaped. So we must be diligent in sowing, which means cultivating disciplined habits of both thinking (setting our minds on what is good) and living (not least in daily meditation in God's Word and in prayer). Natural growth is conditional growth. Be conscientious in securing the conditions, and the growth is bound to follow. If we take care of the seeds, the Holy Spirit will take care of the fruit.

Thirdly, since Christlikeness is gradual in its maturing, we need *patience* to wait. Call it 'impatient patience' if you like, for by patience I do not mean complacency. But every gardener, every farmer, every countryman who lives near the soil knows the need of patience. It is no use trying to change the order of the seasons or the laws of growth which God has established. As James wrote in a different context: 'the farmer waits for the precious fruit of the earth, being patient over it until it receives the early and the late rain' (5:7). He was urging a patient waiting for the coming of the Lord, but he might well have applied the same metaphor to a patient waiting for the fruit of the Spirit. We must fulfil the conditions, as we have seen, but then we must 'wait for the Lord' and look expectantly to him for the fruit to mature, until at length the harvest comes, a ripe Christian character in this life and entire likeness to Christ in the next.

4 The Gifts of the Spirit

In our study of the Holy Spirit we have so far concentrated on his work in the individual believer. The Christian first receives the 'gift' or 'baptism' of the Spirit at the beginning of his new life, and then seeks continuously and increasingly to appropriate the fullness of the Spirit, as a result of which the fruit of the Spirit appears and ripens in his life. The gifts of the Spirit are also given to individual believers, but they are given for the healthy growth of the church.

When the New Testament authors write about the church, they not infrequently contrast its unity and its diversity. Both are due to the work of the Holy Spirit. The church is one because the one Spirit indwells all believers. The church is diverse because the one Spirit distributes different gifts to all believers. Thus the gift of the Spirit (God's gift of the Spirit to us) creates the church's unity, while the gifts of the Spirit (the Holy Spirit's gifts to us) diversify the church's ministry. The same truth may be expressed with reference rather to the grace of God than to the Spirit of God. The church owes its unity to *charis* (grace) and its diversity to *charismata* (gifts of grace).

Four separate lists of spiritual gifts are to be found in the New Testament. The most famous occurs in 1 Corinthians 12. Equally important is Romans 12:3–8. Shorter lists occur in Ephesians 4:7–12 and in 1 Peter 4:10, 11. From these and other passages we must try to discover the nature of spiritual gifts, how many there are, their relation to natural talents, whether they are all miraculous, which gifts are available today, their extent (to whom they are given), their source (where they come from) and their purpose (what they are given for).

The nature of spiritual gifts

Our best starting-point is 1 Corinthians 12:4–6, where Paul states:

> 'Now there are varieties of gifts, but the same Spirit; and there are varieties of service, but the same Lord; and there are varieties of working, but it is the same God who inspires them all in every one.'

The apostle's purpose is to emphasize that, although the gifts are diverse, there is only one Giver. He states this truth three times, each time relating the gifts to a different Person of the Trinity ('the same Spirit', 'the same Lord', 'the same God'). He also uses three different words to denote the gifts themselves. First (verse 4) they are *charismata*, gifts of God's grace. Next (verse 5) they are *diakoniai*, forms of service. Thirdly (verse 6) they are *energēmata*, energies, activities or powers, which the same God 'energizes' or 'inspires' (*energōn*) in everyone. And there are 'varieties' or 'allotments' (*diaireseis*) of each group. Putting the three words together, we might perhaps define spiritual gifts as 'certain capacities, bestowed by God's grace and power, which fit people for specific and corresponding service'. A spiritual gift or *charisma* is, then, neither a capacity by itself, nor a ministry or office by itself, but rather a capacity which qualifies a person for a ministry. More simply it may be regarded either as a gift and the job in which to exercise it, or a job and the gift with which to do it.

We are now ready to pose certain questions regarding

87

these gifts, which will increase our understanding of their nature.

How many different gifts are there?

The interest of some Christians seems to be confined mainly to three gifts, namely 'tongues, prophecy and healing'. But there are obviously more gifts than that exciting trio. I have seen both a book and a booklet entitled *The Nine Gifts of the Spirit*. One appreciates that the authors' motive in limiting the gifts to nine is to draw a parallel with the ninefold fruit of the Spirit, but it is a mistake to restrict the number in this way. Of course it is true that in the first list recorded at the beginning of 1 Corinthians 12 nine gifts are included. It is also true that the second list at the end of the same chapter comprises nine, but only five of these coincide with gifts in the earlier list. So, even in 1 Corinthians 12, thirteen gifts appear to be mentioned. Then there is a list of seven in Romans 12 (five of which do not occur in either list of 1 Corinthians 12), and a list of five in Ephesians 4 (two of which are new), while just two gifts are cited in 1 Peter 4, one of which ('whoever speaks') has not received a specific mention previously. It is not always clear, as we try to compare the five lists, which gift corresponds to which, but it is almost certain that twenty or more distinct gifts are referred to in the New Testament altogether.

Further, there is no reason to suppose that the total of these five lists represents an exhaustive catalogue of all spiritual gifts. We have already noted that in the two lists which occur in the same chapter (1 Cor. 12) only five gifts are repeated, so that each has four new ones, while the list in Ephesians has two new ones not included in either of the 1 Corinthians 12 lists. No single gift occurs in all five lists, and thirteen gifts occur only in one of the five lists. The arrangement seems almost haphazard, as if to draw attention to the fact that each is a limited selection from a much larger total.

Besides, do we not know, from history and experience, of gifts which the Holy Spirit has given to individuals, which are not included in any of the biblical lists? Was not Charles Wesley's ability as a hymnwriter as much a *charisma* as his brother John's gift as an evangelist? And what are we to say about gospel singers, Christian poets, and men and women with outstanding spiritual gifts (I cannot describe them by any other expression) in Christian literature, musical composition, broadcasting and television? Again, only one of the five lists includes 'evangelists'. Is this a comprehensive gift to be claimed by all who engage in any form of evangelism? Or does not our experience of the variety of evangelistic gifts from God suggest that there may be a gift of crusade evangelism, another of home evangelism, another of friendship evangelism, another of casual contact evangelism, another of teaching evangelism, another of literature evangelism, and many more kinds besides?

I venture to suggest that, as with deeper experiences, so with spiritual gifts: our God is a God of rich and colourful diversity. Our human tendency is to try to limit God within arbitrary confines of our own making, to get him 'taped', and to create inflexible stereotypes of both experience and ministry. But the God of creation has made an almost endless variety of fascinating creatures, and among human beings there is an intricate pattern of racial and temperamental types. Scripture suggests that the God of redemption is the same. Once his saving wisdom is depicted as 'many-coloured' (*polupoikilos*, Eph. 3:10). And the same word – though without the prefix – is applied to his grace in bestowing spiritual gifts. We are urged to exercise the gifts we have received 'as good stewards of God's varied grace' (1 Pet. 4:10, *poikilos*, 'variegated' or 'dappled'). The word was applied to marble, embroidered cloth and oriental carpets. The grace of God is like an elaborate tapestry, and the rich diversity of spiritual gifts are the many threads of many colours which are interwoven to make up the beauty of the whole.

In answer to our first question 'how many different gifts are there?' it seems then that we must reply: 'At least twenty are specified in the New Testament, and the living God who loves variety and is a generous giver may well bestow many, many more than that.' Paul makes this point by emphatic repetition as he introduces the subject. In contrast to the one Spirit, he writes, there are *varieties* of gifts, *varieties* of service and *varieties* of working (1 Cor. 12:4–6).

The relation between spiritual gifts and natural talents

What is the relation between spiritual gifts and natural talents? Some would immediately reply 'none', while others have spoken and written as if they thought there was no appreciable difference between them. Both these positions seem to be extreme. There must be some difference, indeed a clear difference, because although the God of creation and providence gives talents to all men and women (so that we speak of people having an artistic 'gift' or a musical 'gift', or being a very 'gifted' personality), yet the God of the new creation, the church, bestows 'spiritual gifts' only upon his redeemed people. It is spiritual gifts which differentiate the members of Christ's body, each member of the body having a different gift or function. Nevertheless, we should be slow to deduce from this fact that there is no link whatever between the two. A number of reasons should make us pause.

First, the same God is God of creation and of new creation, working out through both his perfect will. This divine will is eternal. God told Jeremiah at the time of his call to the prophetic office: 'Before I formed you in the womb I knew you, and before you were born I consecrated you; I appointed you a prophet to the nations' (Je. 1:5). Paul had the same conviction about himself and his vocation as an apostle. The God who revealed his Son to him was 'he who had set me apart before I was born, and had called me through his grace' (Gal. 1:15, 16). Notice that both these verses contain more than a time reference, that before the births of Jeremiah and Paul God knew what was going to happen to them. What is asserted is that already before their births God had consecrated them or set them apart for the particular ministry to which he would later call them. Surely then we cannot suppose that there was no bridge between the two halves of their life? Would it not be more in keeping with the God of the Bible to suppose that he gave them an actual endowment *before* their call (genetic conditioning, we might say in modern terms), which came to life and came into use only *after* it? God was active in both halves of their lives and perfectly fitted the two together. Similarly, all the biblical authors were first prepared by God's providence in terms of their temperament, upbringing and experience, and then inspired by the Holy Spirit to communicate a message which was entirely appropriate to the kind of person they were.

If it be objected that what may have been true of prophets and apostles is not necessarily true of ordinary Christians today, I would reply that Scripture suggests the contrary. For God's gracious purpose for each of us is eternal. It was formed and even 'given' to us in Christ 'before eternal times' (2 Tim. 1:9, literally); God chose us to be holy and destined us to be his sons through Jesus Christ 'before the foundation of the world' (Eph. 1:4, 5); and the good works for which we were re-created in Christ are precisely those 'which God prepared beforehand'. This fundamental truth that God has planned the end from the beginning should warn us against too facile a discontinuity between nature and grace, between our pre-conversion and post-conversion life.

There is a second reason for expecting a link between natural and spiritual gifts. Several *charismata* are not only non-miraculous but positively mundane. They are spiritual gifts of a material nature. Perhaps the most striking examples are the last three in the list Paul gives in Romans 12:

> 'he who contributes, in liberality; he who gives aid, with zeal; he who does acts of mercy, with cheerfulness' (12:8).

Now there can be no doubt that these belong to the category of *charismata*. The word itself occurs at the beginning of verse 6. The whole list comes under the 'one-body-many-members' metaphor (verses 4, 5) as in 1 Corinthians 12. And all seven gifts in the Romans 12 catalogue are presented in an almost identical pattern.

What, then, are these last three gifts? The middle one of the trio is ambiguous in the Greek, for it could mean 'he who gives aid' (as in RSV), but it could also mean 'he who rules' or 'takes the lead', and is so used of church leaders and presbyters in 1 Thessalonians 5:12 and 1 Timothy 5: 17. There is no ambiguity about the other two gifts, however. One ('he who contributes') refers to giving money and is specifically used in Ephesians 4:28 of giving 'to those in need', while the other is 'he who does acts of mercy'. Now unbelievers can (and do) both give money to needy people and perform acts of mercy. So in what sense can these be regarded as 'spiritual gifts' bestowed by God exclusively on his people? It seems unlikely, to say the least, that one of the spiritual gifts in question is a sudden post-conversion windfall of money! No, I think we must agree that the *wherewithal* (the money to give, the strength to serve) is already there in these people's pre-conversion days. So what is new, what turns their natural endowment into a spiritual gift, must lie in the realm of their *objective* (the causes they serve and to which they give) and of their *motive* (the incentives which guide them). It is here, at any rate, that Paul lays his emphasis. There is to be no grudging, reluctant mood, he says. The giver of money is to exercise his gift 'with generosity' (verse 8, literally), and the one who does merciful deeds 'with cheerfulness'.

A rather similar link between pre-conversion natural talent and post-conversion spiritual gift may also exist in two of the earlier *charismata* which Paul mentions in Romans 12, namely 'he who teaches' (verse 7) and 'he who exhorts' (verse 8). It is obvious what 'teaching' means. The verb for 'exhort' (*parakaleō*), however, has several shades of meaning ranging from 'begging' and 'entreating' to 'encouraging', 'comforting' and 'consoling'. Both verbs may refer to different aspects of a public speaking ministry, instruction on the one hand and exhortation on the other. Certainly 'exhortation' (*paraklēsis*) can be given formally in speech (Acts 13:15) and in writing (Heb. 13:22). Nevertheless, *paraklēsis* is a wider concept and includes the kind of encouragement and comfort which personal friendship, sympathy and love can bring. Now both instruction and encouragement are given by non-Christian people. In the secular world we meet many who are (as we say) 'born teachers', and others whose great gift is their understanding, their approachability, their sensitivity, as a result of which they cheer people up and encourage them on their way. So what can be the difference between non-Christian teachers and encouragers on the one hand, and Christians with these spiritual gifts on the other?

In view of what has been written above about the God of nature and of grace, is it not *a priori* unlikely that God will give a spiritual gift of teaching to a believer who in pre-conversion days could not teach for toffee, or a spiritual gift of encouragement to a brother or sister who by temperament is unsympathetic and unfriendly? It would not be impossible to God. But would it not be more in harmony with the God of the Bible, whose plans are eternal, to suppose that his spiritual gifts dovetail with his natural endowments? And that (for example) a 'son of encouragement' such as Barnabas (Acts 4:36), who exercised his particular ministry both by generous giving (verse 37) and by personal friendship (*e.g.* Acts 9:26, 27; 11:25, 26), was already that kind of person, at least potentially, by creation?

In this case we must look for the peculiarities of the spiritual gifts of teaching and encouragement in the heightening, the intensification, the 'Christianizing' of a natural endowment already present, or at least latent. Thus, a man may be a gifted teacher before his conversion, and may after it be given the *charisma* of teaching to enable him to expound with insight, clarity and relevance. Or he may have a sympathetic disposition by nature, but after conversion be given the spiritual gift of 'encouragement' to enable him to exercise a specifically Christian ministry of 'encouragement in Christ' (Phil. 2:1), both by his Christian instruction (*e.g.* 1 Thes. 4:18; Tit. 1:9) and by the warmth and strength of his Christian faith (Rom. 1:12). In all these last references the words *parakaleō* or *paraklēsis* occur.

So the biblical evidence warns us not to draw too hard and fast a line of demarcation between natural and spiritual gifts. In his great seventeenth-century book, *Pneumatologia* or *A Discourse Concerning the Holy Spirit*, John Owen distinguished thus between two sorts of spiritual gift – 'such as exceeded all the powers and faculties of men's minds' and 'such as consisted in extraordinary improvements of the faculties of the mind of men'.[1]

Are all spiritual gifts miraculous gifts?

Some will be surprised by the question, because they have never thought of all *charismata* as involving a miracle. Yet the question needs to be asked, because some now give the impression that the word 'charismatic' is more or less synonymous with 'miraculous'.

Our answer to the question must begin with the repetition that some gifts, far from being miraculous, appear to be quite ordinary, even prosaic. There is nothing miraculous

[1] 4th Edition (Richard Baynes, London, 1835), p. 310.

about the gifts of teaching and encouraging, giving money and doing acts of mercy. Nor is there any obvious reason from the words themselves why we should suppose 'the utterance of wisdom', 'the utterance of knowledge' or 'faith' (1 Cor. 12:8, 9) to be or to include miracles. Nothing in the text or context suggests this. The natural interpretation would be that they refer to a special measure of wisdom and knowledge (together with a gift of expressing it) and a special degree of faith not, of course, for justification or sanctification, but for some particular kind of ministry. To take an Old Testament example, Solomon was endowed with the gift of wisdom, and the heroes of Hebrews 11 with the gift of faith.

Again, both Paul and Peter call 'serving' a spiritual gift (Rom. 12:7; 1 Pet. 4:11). It is the common verb *diakoneō* and could refer to any kind of ministry, pastoral or (more probably) practical. *Ho diakonōn* is the waiter who serves at meals (Lk. 22:26f.), and the same word is used of Martha's domestic chores (Lk. 10:40). Next, Paul refers in 1 Corinthians 12:28 to two *charismata* which the RSV translates 'helpers' (*antilēmpseis*) and 'administrators' (*kubernēseis*). The first word occurs nowhere else in the New Testament, but is correctly rendered 'helps' or possibly 'helpful deeds'. It seems to be another general word like 'service'. *Kubernēsis*, on the other hand, means 'administration', and the Arndt-Gingrich Lexicon adds that 'the plural indicates proofs of ability to hold a leading position in the church'. The cognate word *kubernētēs* is the 'steersman', 'pilot', even 'captain' of a ship (Acts 27:11), and came to be applied metaphorically in classical Greek to people in leading secular positions, for example, the governor of a city. *Kubernēsis* would seem, then, to be the gift of guiding or governing others, including perhaps organizing ability to take responsibility for some part of the church's programme, or the leadership to take the chair at a meeting and 'steer' the committee's proceedings with wisdom.

What, then, about the miraculous gifts? 'The working of miracles' and 'workers of miracles' proclaim themselves as involving miracle, and so probably do 'gifts of healing' and 'healers', together with 'various kinds of tongues', and 'the interpretation of tongues' (1 Cor. 12:9, 10, 28, 29). Assuming these to be miraculous gifts, are they still bestowed today? It is strange that people are often quick to take sides on this issue, with a simple 'yes' or 'no', without first enquiring whether there is a biblical doctrine of miracles in the light of which the question may be considered and answered. For I venture to say that the naïve 'yes' and 'no' answers are both extreme positions. To begin with, a dogmatic 'no', with perhaps the addition of 'miracles don't happen today' or (worse) 'miracles can't happen', is an impossible position for a biblical Christian to hold. The God we believe in is the free and sovereign Creator of the universe. He upholds everything by the word of his power. All nature is subservient to him. He not only *can* work miracles but *has* done so. Who are we to circumscribe his power and tell him what he may or may not do?

The opposite position seems equally untenable, however. In its most extreme form it is the view that almost everything God does is miraculous. But a miracle by definition is an extraordinary event, a creative deviation from God's normal and natural ways of working. If miracles were to become commonplace they would cease to be miracles. Yet some Christians detect the activity of God only in the miraculous. They have then turned him into a kind of magician. There is an urgent need for all of us to grasp the biblical revelation of the living God who works primarily in nature not in supernature, in history not in miracle. He is the most high God who rules the kingdom of men (Dn. 4:32), with whom 'the nations are like a drop from a bucket' and who 'takes up the isles like fine dust' (Is. 40:15), who 'executes judgment, putting down one and lifting up another' (Ps. 75:7). It is he also who causes his sun to rise and sends the rain (Mt. 5:45), who maintains the regularity of the seasons (Gn. 8:22; Acts 14:17), who rules the raging of the sea (Ps. 89:9), who feeds the birds of the air and clothes the flowers of the field (Mt. 6:26, 30), and has the breath of man in his hand (Dn. 5:23).

Once we begin to see the living God ceaselessly at work through the processes of history and nature, we shall begin (for example) to recognize that *all* healing is divine healing, whether without the use of means or through the use of physical, psychological or surgical means. The former should properly be termed 'miraculous healing', while the latter is non-miraculous, but both are equally 'divine healing'.

A less extreme form of this second position is to hold that, even if not everything God does is miraculous, nevertheless he intends miracles to be as regular a feature of our life and ministry today as they were in the ministry of our Lord and his apostles. But this also cannot be seriously maintained by those whose doctrine of miracles is derived from Scripture. For although the Bible contains a number of miracle-stories, it is not exclusively a book of miracles any more than the God of the Bible is exclusively a God of miracles. Large tracts of biblical history contain no record of any miracle. John the Baptist, whom Jesus said was the greatest man of the old dispensation, is specifically said to have performed no miracles (Jn. 10:41). In fact when we seek to discover where the biblical miracles are, we find that they cluster in Scripture like stars in the night sky. There are four main constellations. They cluster first round Moses (the plagues of Egypt, the crossing of the Red Sea, the manna and the water, *etc.*), next round Elijah, Elisha and the prophets, thirdly round the Lord Jesus himself and fourthly round the apostles. Now these are the four main epochs of revelation – the law, the prophets, the Lord and the apostles. And the major purpose of miracles was to authenticate each fresh stage of revelation. For example, the uniqueness of Moses as a prophet ('whom the Lord knew face to face') was confirmed by the uniqueness of his miracles ('none like him for all the signs and the wonders which the Lord sent him to do' Dt. 34:10, 11). Similarly, the ministry of the Lord Jesus was 'attested ... by God with mighty works and wonders and signs which God did through him ...' (Acts 2:22), while God also bore witness to the message of the apostolic eyewitnesses 'by signs and wonders and various miracles and by gifts[2] of the Holy Spirit distributed according to his own will' (Heb. 2:3, 4). It is correct, therefore, to refer to the book of Acts as 'the Acts of the Apostles', for all the miracles Luke records in this book were performed by apostles (*cf.* Acts 2:43; 5:12), and the only two exceptions were by men whom the apostles had personally commissioned by the laying-on of hands (6:8; 8:6, 7). Paul's miracles, too, were described by him as 'the signs of a true apostle' (2 Cor. 12:12).[3]

What, then, should be our response to miraculous claims today? It should be neither a stubborn incredulity ('but miracles don't happen today') nor an uncritical gullibility ('of course! miracles are happening all the time'), but rather a spirit of open-minded enquiry: 'I don't expect miracles as a commonplace today, because the special reve-

---

[2] The word is not *charismata* but *merismoi*, 'distributions', and may refer to the Spirit's distribution of powers, as the context suggests, rather than of gifts.

[3] The words attributed to the risen Lord that certain 'signs' will 'accompany those who believe' occur in the so-called 'longer ending' of Mark's Gospel (16:17, 18), which appears in modern Bibles as a small-print appendix. An alternative 'shorter ending' is also usually printed. Most scholars are of the opinion, on the basis of the poor manuscript attestation of these endings, either that Mark's Gospel ended abruptly with verse 8 or (more probably) that it originally had an ending which included the resurrection appearances of Jesus but that this ending was accidentally lost. This would explain the alternative conclusions which later hands provided. It would at the very least be extremely precarious to base a belief in the normality of miracles on this longer ending, since it is almost certainly not authentic Mark and therefore not authentic Jesus.

lation they were given to authenticate is complete; but of course God is sovereign and God is free, and there may well be particular situations in which he pleases to perform them.'

Are all the spiritual gifts of the Bible given today?

It has already been suggested that the four biblical lists may well not be exhaustive, and that there may be some spiritual gifts available today which are not included in any list. Now the opposite point must also be made, that not all the twenty or more gifts which *are* listed are available. Leaving aside the question of the miraculous gifts, which has already been considered, we must approach the question whether there are 'apostles' and 'prophets' in today's church. Among those who begin with the presupposition that all the *charismata* mentioned in the New Testament are readily available, the continued existence of apostles and prophets is taken for granted. Such Christians tend to say and write that there is 'no biblical evidence whatever' that any gifts would ever be withdrawn. But, on the contrary, there *is* evidence for the very thing for which they say there is none.

The word 'apostle' is probably used in three senses in the New Testament. In one text only it seems to be applied to all Christians, namely when Jesus said that 'he who is sent' (Greek *apostolos*) is not greater than he who sent him (Jn. 13:16). In the general sense that all of us are sent into the world by Christ and thus share in the apostolic mission of the church (Jn. 17:18; 20:21), all of us are in the broadest term 'apostles'. But since this can apply to all Christians it is not a *charisma* given only to some.

Secondly, the word is used at least twice to describe 'apostles of the churches' (2 Cor. 8:23; Phil. 2:25), messengers sent on particular errands from one church to another. In this sense the word might be applied to missionaries and other Christians sent on special missions. But this is plainly not the sense which the *charisma* 'apostle' bears. For what is immediately noteworthy about the two lists in which 'apostles' occurs is that on both occasions it heads the list (1 Cor. 12:28, 29; Eph. 4:11), and that in the Corinthian list the first three gifts are enumerated ('first, second, third') with apostles as 'first'. The gift of apostleship which is thus given precedence must refer, therefore, to that small and special group of men who were 'apostles of Christ', consisting of the Twelve (Lk. 6:12, 13), together with Paul (*e.g.* Gal. 1:1), probably James the Lord's brother (Gal. 1:19) and possibly one or two others. They were unique in being eyewitnesses of the historic Jesus, especially of the risen Lord (Acts 1:21, 22; 1 Cor. 9:1; 15:8, 9), in being personally appointed and authorized by Christ (Mk. 3:14) and in being specially inspired by the Holy Spirit for their teaching ministry (*e.g.* Jn. 14:25, 26; 16:12–15). In this primary sense, therefore, in which they appear in the lists, they have no successors, in the very nature of the case, although there are no doubt 'apostles' today in the secondary sense of 'missionaries'.

What about prophets? Of course many times in the church's history there have been claims to prophetic inspiration. But are the claims true? It depends largely on our definition of 'prophecy' and 'prophet'. The biblical understanding, dating back to Old Testament days, is that a prophet was an organ of divine revelation, to whom the word of the Lord came, and who therefore spoke the very words of God (*e.g.* Ex. 4:12; 7:1, 2; Je. 1:4–9; 23:16, 18, 22, 28). In this meaning of the term, which is the essential biblical meaning, I think we must say that there are no more prophets, for God's self-revelation was completed in Christ and in the apostolic witness to Christ, and the canon of Scripture has long since been closed. Moreover, 'prophets' come second to apostles in the Ephesian and Corinthian lists mentioned above, and 'apostles and prophets' are bracketed in several texts and said to be the foundation (because of their teaching) on which the church is built (Eph. 2:20; 3:5). Now the simplest knowledge of architectural construction is enough to tell us that once the foundation of a building is laid and the superstructure is being built, the foundation cannot be laid again. So in the primary sense of 'prophets', as vehicles of direct and fresh revelation, it seems we must say that this *charisma* is no longer given. There is no longer anyone in the church who may dare to say 'The word of the Lord came to me, saying . . .' or 'Thus says the Lord'.

It has been argued, however, that 'prophet' may be used in other and lesser senses. Some think there may be men today like the prophet Agabus (Acts 11:28; 21:10, 11), whose function is not to add to revelation but to foretell some future event. This is possible. But both church history and personal experience make me cautious. Nothing brought such discredit on Edward Irving and his 'Catholic Apostolic Church' towards the beginning of the last century than the fact that the prophecies of the 'prophetesses' did not come true. My own observations confirm this, for I have myself heard several unfulfilled predictions, which have led those concerned either to dishonesty or to disillusion. Others suggest that a prophetic ministry is one which interprets political events or comments on social issues (as did the Old Testament prophets), but it is difficult to isolate this aspect of their work from their divine inspiration. Others again interpret the gift of prophecy as the gift of Scripture exposition or of preaching, or of 'upbuilding and encouragement and consolation' (1 Cor. 14:3). Thus Abraham Kuyper wrote: 'by prophecy St Paul designates animated preaching, wherein the preacher feels himself cheered and inspired by the Holy Spirit.'[4]

Yet all these interpretations fall short of the high biblical view of prophecy. For in Scripture the prophet is primarily neither the predictor of the future, nor the political commentator, nor the lively preacher, nor even the bringer of

[4] A. Kuyper, *The Work of the Holy Spirit*, 1888 (Funk and Wagnalls, London and New York, 1900), p. 187.

encouragement, but the mouthpiece of God, the organ of fresh revelation. It seems to be in that sense that Paul brackets 'apostles and prophets' as the most important of all *charismata* (Eph. 2:20; 3:5; 4:11; 1 Cor. 12:28); and in that sense (whatever may be said about subsidiary meanings and ministries) we must say they no longer exist in the church. God's way of teaching in today's church is not by fresh revelation but by exposition of his revelation completed in Christ and in Scripture.

The word 'charismatic'

We have been examining the nature of the *charismata*, and have been asking and answering certain questions about them. It all leads me to register a mild protest against several misuses of the English adjective 'charismatic' which misrepresent the nature of the *charismata*.

Some theologians oppose the terms 'charismatic' and 'institutional' when talking about the Christian ministry. They call pastors and teachers (like bishops and presbyters) 'institutional', while prophets are 'charismatic', the former being appointed by the church and the latter directly by God himself. But this is (at least partially) a false distinction. It is true that 'apostles and prophets' were called by God without any formal authorization by the church. But the church has no right to authorize men whom God has not called. According to Scripture, pastors and teachers are just as much 'charismatic' as prophets (Eph. 4:11), and no man should ever be appointed to an office by the church who has not been already called and gifted by God. The New Testament never contemplates such a grotesque anomaly as a man in a ministry without the *charisma* to qualify him for the ministry. John Owen expressed it admirably: 'The Church has no power to call any person to the office of the ministry, where Christ hath not gone before it in the designation of that person by an endowment of spiritual gifts.'[5]

[5] John Owen, *op. cit.*, p. 315.

One can go further still and say (for example) that the New Testament draws no distinction between 'the gift of teaching' and 'the gift of teacher' (*e.g.* 1 Cor. 12:28; Rom. 12:7; Eph. 4:11). The *charisma* consists of a combination of office and gift.

It has become fashionable in recent years for journalists to write of 'charismatic' leaders, or of politicians or artists with 'charisma'. When they use it, the word seems to describe a mixture of charm and genius. The so-called 'charismatic' figure has a scintillating personality. But there is no justification for the application of the word to secular stars who do not confess Jesus as Lord. The false impression is also given that the New Testament *charismata* are all spectacular gifts, whereas we have seen that to do hidden works of mercy, generosity and administration may be equally 'charismatic' in the true biblical sense.

Thirdly, there is the contemporary 'charismatic movement', to which reference has already been made. Speaking for myself, I use this expression as a courtesy to those who prefer it to any other; but I do so reluctantly, because it seems to me seriously misleading. For this is to apply to a group of Christians within the church the epithet 'charismatic' which properly belongs to the whole church. The whole church is a charismatic community. It is the Body of Christ, whose members function as a result of their gifts (*charismata*).

The extent of spiritual gifts: to whom are they given?
Having tried to define what spiritual gifts are – in their rich variety, their relation to natural endowments, and their inclusion of the mundane as well as the sensational – it is time to enquire about their distribution. To whom are they given? Our immediate answer must be that if there is a wide diversity of gifts there is a wide distribution also. *Charismata* are not the prerogative of a select few. On the

contrary, the New Testament gives us warrant to affirm that every Christian has at least one spiritual gift or capacity for service, however dormant and unused his gift may be. The evidence for this assertion is twofold.

First, all four chapters in which spiritual gifts are listed contain a direct statement to this effect:

'I bid *every one* among you . . . to think with sober judgment, each according to the measure of faith which God has assigned him . . . Having gifts that differ . . ., let us use them' (Rom. 12:3–6).

'All these are inspired by one and the same Spirit, who apportions to *each one* individually as he wills' (1 Cor. 12:11).

'But grace was given to *each* of us according to the measure of Christ's gift . . .' (Eph. 4:7).

'As *each* has received a gift, employ it for one another, as good stewards of God's varied grace' (1 Pet. 4:10).

The italicized word in each verse is either *pas* ('every') or *hekastos* ('each'). It is surely very striking to observe that gifts are more than widespread; they are universal.

Secondly, there is the body metaphor, Paul's favourite representation of the church as the body of Christ. The church resembles the human body in that both are co-ordinated systems consisting of many members, each with a distinctive function. It is significant that in all three passages in which Paul refers to spiritual gifts (Rom. 12; 1 Cor. 12 and Eph. 4) he develops this body metaphor. It seems that in his mind the body of Christ and the *charismata* belong necessarily together. And in two of his three expositions the link between them is plain. His argument is partly that, as in the human body, so in Christ's body, each organ or member has *some* function, and partly that each has a *different* function.

'For as in one body we have many members, and all the members do not have the same function, so we, though many, are one body in Christ, and individually members one of another. Having gifts (*charismata*) that differ according to the grace given to us, let us use them ...' (Rom. 12:4–6).

'For just as the body is one and has many members, and all the members of the body, though many, are one body, so it is with Christ. ... For the body does not consist of one member but of many. ... Now you are the body of Christ and individually members of it' (1 Cor. 12:12, 14, 27).

This fact, that every Christian has a gift and therefore a responsibility, and that no Christian is passed by and left without endowment, is fundamental to the New Testament doctrine of the church. It should also transform the life of Christians and of churches. For the traditional image of the local church is of an overworked pastor, assisted perhaps by a small nucleus of dedicated workers, while the majority of members make little or no contribution to the church's life and work. It conjures up the picture rather of a bus (one driver, many drowsy passengers) than of a body (all members active, each contributing a particular activity to the health and effectiveness of the whole). Indeed, I do not doubt that a false image of the church is one of the main reasons for the growth of the 'charismatic movement'. This movement is a protest against clericalism (the clerical suppression of the laity) and a plea for the liberation of the laity for those responsible leadership roles for which God has gifted them.

Many local churches (and especially their pastors) complain that the congregation lacks gifted lay leadership, and this is the standard excuse for attempting little and for preserving the control over what little is attempted firmly in the hands of the pastor. But Scripture addresses each local church with the same words which Paul used to the Corinthians: 'you are the body of Christ.' Here then are Scripture and appearances at variance with each other, appearances indicating that the congregation is destitute of gifts, while Scripture says, 'Nonsense! It cannot be. You are the body of Christ!' Such a conflict between God's Word and man's assessment precipitates a crisis of faith. If we take God at his word, then we are committed to believe that he has endowed, or at least is willing to endow, each local church with all the gifts it needs for its life, health, growth and work. Our duty is to pray that God will raise up gifted workers; to be constantly on the look-out for gifts which are either consciously buried or unconsciously neglected; to encourage people to exercise their God-given gifts (*cf.* 1 Tim. 4:14; 2 Tim. 1:6); and to ensure that they have opportunities to do so. Of course there is a place for volunteers who offer their services; but it is more healthy and more biblical for the church oversight to be alert to the ways God is equipping and calling his people to serve.

I remember being struck at the European Congress on Evangelism, which was held in Amsterdam in 1971, by a wise word spoken by Jan van Capelleveen, journalist, broadcaster, and Information Secretary of the Netherlands Bible Society. He suggested that we should 'make an inventory of the spiritual opportunities and spiritual gifts of the local church'. That is, a group from every church should take time and trouble to consider what work God is calling them to undertake and what resources he has given them (or would need to give them) to do it. This identifying of goals and this matching of resources to goals may be elementary principles of modern business management; but the Bible taught them long before management studies were even thought of! At any rate, nothing is better calculated to deliver a local church from clericalism or to promote the mobilization of its membership than the recognition of the simple biblical truths that the church is Christ's body and that every member of the body has a function to perform. It is in this sense, as we have seen, that the whole church is a 'charismatic community', for every member of the community has a *charisma*, and in some cases more than one.

The source of spiritual gifts: where do they come from?

We have defined the diverse nature and the widespread distribution of *charismata*. We now have to emphasize that they come from God. Spiritual gifts are God's gifts. The New Testament expresses this in various ways.

First, spiritual gifts are gifts of *God's grace*. The Greek words themselves indicate this plainly. *Charismata* are the endowments of *charis*, that is, of God's undeserved favour. Consider these texts:

'Having gifts (*charismata*) that differ according to the grace (*charis*) given to us, let us use them' (Rom. 12:6).

'But grace (*charis*) was given to each of us according to the measure of Christ's gift (*dōrea*)' (Eph. 4:7).

'As each has received a gift (*charisma*), employ it for one another, as good stewards of God's varied grace (*charis*)' (1 Pet. 4:10).

In order to feel the force of this, it may be helpful to remind ourselves that the word *charisma* is applied in the New Testament not only to spiritual gifts, but also to salvation. For example, 'the wages of sin is death, but the free gift (*charisma*) of God is eternal life in Christ Jesus our Lord' (Rom. 6:23). We are accustomed to ascribing our salvation to God's sheer and undeserved mercy, and nothing is more conducive to humility than this fact. Yet the *charismata* which are given for service are just as much the free and unmerited bestowal of God as is the *charisma* of eternal life. So in this area too there is room neither for jealousy nor for boasting.

107

Secondly, spiritual gifts are gifts of *God's Spirit*. The twelfth chapter of 1 Corinthians opens literally with the words: 'Now concerning the spirituals' or 'concerning the spiritual things' (*peri de tōn pneumatikōn*). Although the RSV translates it 'now concerning spiritual gifts', it will be noted that the word is not *charismata*. Perhaps Paul deliberately uses this vaguer expression because he is going on to write of the work of the Spirit in several spheres, in illumining our minds to confess Jesus as Lord (verse 3) and in uniting us to Christ's body when we are baptized with him and drink of him (verse 13), as well as in endowing us with spiritual gifts. The phrases 'the Spirit', 'the Spirit of God', 'the Holy Spirit', 'the same Spirit', 'the one Spirit' and 'one and the same Spirit' together occur eleven times in the first thirteen verses. So the emphasis is beyond question.

Nevertheless, in verses 4 to 6 (as we noted earlier) there is a conscious reference to all three Persons of the Trinity, 'the same God', 'the same Lord' and 'the same Spirit'. Further, in Romans 12 and 1 Peter 4 God the Father is the author of spiritual gifts, while in Ephesians 4 they are the gifts of the ascended Christ, the head of the church, who in fulfilment of prophecy 'gave gifts to men' (verses 7–11). It seems that, although the Holy Spirit is the executive of the Godhead and what God does today he does by his Spirit, nevertheless, as with deeper experiences so with spiritual gifts, we should not ascribe them exclusively to the Spirit, but remember that the three Persons of the Trinity are involved.

Thirdly, spiritual gifts are gifts of *God's sovereignty*. In Ephesians 4 Christ at his ascension is represented as a victorious general, leading a host of captives and distributing gifts from the booty. The gifts are free and the giving sovereign. This is further stated in 1 Corinthians 12:11: 'one and the same Spirit . . . apportions to each one individually as he wills.'

True, we are permitted, indeed commanded, to 'desire

the higher gifts' and to desire them 'earnestly' (1 Cor. 12:31). Presumably this earnest desire is related to 'the measure of faith which God has assigned' us (Rom. 12:3), and we are encouraged in Scripture to pray for an increase of faith. Nevertheless, the apportionment of gifts lies not in our will but in the will of the sovereign Holy Spirit himself. So the *charismata* originate in the gracious will of God, and are bestowed by him through the Holy Spirit.

The apostle elaborates the consequences of this fact at some length (1 Cor. 12:14-26). His argument is that if the Holy Spirit distributes spiritual gifts according to his gracious and sovereign will, then there is no possible justification for either envy or vanity. How can we depreciate our own gift and look with envy on the gifts of others if God has given us our gifts according to his grace and will? Equally, how can we despise other people's gifts and compare them unfavourably with ours if God has given them their gifts according to his grace and will? We shall consider how he handles the opposite sins of self-depreciation and self-importance.

First, self-depreciation (verses 15-20). With amusing vividness he makes the various parts of the human body talk. The foot must not disparage itself and say, 'Look at me! I'm no use. I can't pick things up and perform complicated manoeuvres like the versatile hand. I'm just a clumsy old foot.' Similarly, the ear must not belittle itself and say, 'Look at me! I'm no use either. I can't see anything, whether shapes or colours. I'm blind. All I can do is hear noises.' But such self-deprecatory remarks are stupid and they do not make either foot or ear 'any less a part of the body'. For if the whole body were one colossal eye, how could it hear anything? And if it were one enormous ear, what would happen to its sense of smell? No, the body needs to hear as well as see, and to smell as well as hear. So God has 'arranged the organs in the body', each with a distinctive function, 'as he chose'. If he had not done so, there would have been no body. 'As it is,' however, 'there are many parts, yet one body.' So no organ has good cause to depreciate itself.

The opposite sin is self-importance (verses 21–26). The eye cannot despise the hand or dismiss it contemptuously, saying, 'I don't need you. You're only a hand. You can grasp and hold things, it's true. But you're useless, for you can't see.' Again, the head has no right to look down from its superior height to the feet and say smugly, 'I don't need you! You're just a couple of old feet in clodhoppers. I concede that you can move clumsily about. But I'm the brainbox. I house the central nervous system. I do the thinking and the planning and the deciding. I can get along all right without you.' Paul not only denies this kind of patronizing talk, but contradicts it. 'On the contrary,' he says, 'God has so composed the body' as to make its weaker parts indispensable and to give its less presentable parts greater honour.

To recapitulate, the voice of self-depreciation says, 'I'm no good; you don't need me,' while the voice of self-importance says, 'You're no good; I don't need you.' But the voice of God says, 'You need each other.' The gifts which God has given to us and the gifts which he has given to others are all important and necessary. Together they constitute the complete and healthy body of Christ, all of whose members are functioning properly.

Only when we give up depreciating ourselves and others, and instead recognize the gifts of God, will there be 'no discord in the body' (verse 25). God hates discord. His will is rather 'that the members may have the same care for one another', sharing in each other's sufferings and joys. And the great truth which alone can deliver us from envy and vanity is that spiritual gifts are God's gifts, distributed by his grace and according to his will. In John Owen's delightful phrase, they are the 'arbitrary largesses' of God.[6] So we

[6] John Owen, *op. cit.*, p. 324.

must not devalue them, whether they are given to us or to others.

The purpose of spiritual gifts: what they are given for?

God's gifts are given to be used. The organs of the human body are functional. Similarly, the members of Christ's body are to exercise their gifts. We are 'stewards of God's varied grace', and are commanded to be 'good stewards' (1 Pet. 4:10). 'Having gifts,' wrote Paul, 'let us use them' (Rom. 12:6). But how should we use them?

Much misunderstanding surrounds the purpose for which God distributes spiritual gifts in the church. Some speak of them as 'love gifts', as if their main purpose is to enrich the recipient and we are to use them for our own benefit. Others think of them as 'worship gifts', as if their main purpose is the worship of God and their main sphere of operation is the conduct of public worship. But Scripture asserts that they are 'service gifts', whose primary purpose is to 'edify' or build up the church.

The apostles Paul and Peter both stress the unselfish use of God's gifts in the service of other people, indeed of the whole church:

'To each is given the manifestation of the Spirit *for the common good*' (1 Cor. 12:7).

'As each has received a gift, employ it *for one another*' (1 Pet. 4:10).

Thus spiritual gifts are given not to help, comfort and strengthen ourselves (the recipients) but others. This is the meaning of 'edification' (*cf.* Eph. 4:12, 16).

This too is the reason why some gifts are more valuable than others. No gift is to be despised, as we have seen. At the same time we are to desire earnestly 'the higher gifts' (1 Cor. 12:31). How, then, are we to assess their relative importance? The only possible answer to this is 'according to the degree to which they edify'. Since all the *charismata* are given for the building up of individual Christians and the whole church, the more they build the greater their value. Paul is crystal-clear about this. 'Since you are eager for manifestations of the Spirit,' he writes, 'strive to excel in building up the church' (1 Cor. 14:12).

By this criterion the teaching gifts have the highest value, for nothing builds up Christians like God's truth. It is not surprising, therefore, to find a teaching gift or gifts at the top of each of the five New Testament lists. The apostles' insistence on the priority of teaching has considerable relevance to the contemporary church. All over the world the churches are spiritually undernourished owing to the shortage of biblical expositors. In areas where there are mass movements they are crying out for teachers to instruct converts. Because of the dearth of teachers it is sad to see so many people preoccupied with, and even distracted by, gifts of lesser importance.

Probably at this point something needs to be said about 'tongues', a gift much emphasized by some. A question-mark still stands over the contemporary phenomenon known as tongue-speaking, whether it is identical with the New Testament gift. It is clear that on the Day of Pentecost the Spirit-filled believers were speaking 'in other tongues', *i.e.* in foreign languages, 'as the Spirit gave them utterance', and that all these languages were intelligible to groups in the crowd (Acts 2:4–11). There is a strong theological and linguistic presumption that the phenomenon referred to in 1 Corinthians is the same. First, the Greek phrases are almost exactly the same, and one of the first rules of biblical interpretation is that identical expressions have an identical meaning. Secondly, the noun *glōssa* has only two known meanings, namely the organ in the mouth and a language. There is no linguistic warrant for the NEB rendering 'ecstatic utterance'. This is not a translation but an interpretation. Similarly the verb for the 'interpretation of tongues' means the translation of languages. Thirdly, the whole thrust of I Corinthians 14 is to discourage the cult of unintelligibility as a childish thing: 'Brethren, do not be children in your thinking . . ., but in thinking be mature' (verse 20). The God of the Bible is a rational God and does not delight in irrationality or unintelligibility.

This interpretation raises a few exegetical difficulties, which have led some to distinguish sharply between 'tongues' in the Acts and 'tongues' in I Corinthians. But the difficulties are small in comparison with the strength of the argument that the phenomenon is the same, not an unintelligible ecstatic utterance but an intelligible language – intelligible, that is, to some present (as on the Day of Pentecost); it would of course need to be 'interpreted' or 'translated' in a multilingual port like Corinth for the benefit of those who spoke another language. If the gift is essentially linguistic, one can understand better why Paul puts it at the bottom of the list, and why it is not even mentioned in the three other lists. It is true that he says 'I want you all to speak in tongues' (much as Moses said 'Would that all the Lord's people were prophets', Nu. 11:29), because all God's gifts are good and desirable, but in itself (apart, that is, from the content spoken) it does not have a particular ability to edify.

What, then, about the contemporary practice of private tongue-speaking as an aid to personal devotion? Many are claiming to discover through it a new degree of fluency in their approach to God. Others have spoken of a kind of 'psychic release' which they have found liberating and which one would not want to deny them. On the other hand, it needs to be said (from 1 Cor. 14) that if Paul completely forbids public tongue-speaking without interpretation, he strongly discourages private tongue-speaking if the speaker does not understand what he is saying. Verse 13 is often overlooked: 'He who speaks in a tongue should pray for the power to interpret'. Otherwise his mind will be 'unfruitful' or unproductive. So what is he to do? Paul asks himself. His reply is that he will pray and sing 'with the Spirit', but he will do so 'with the mind also'. It is clear that he simply cannot contemplate Christian prayer and praise in which the mind is not actively engaged.

Some readers will no doubt respond that in the early verses of 1 Corinthians 14 the apostle contrasts prophecy and tongue-speaking, states that the prophet 'edifies the church' while the tongue-speaker 'edifies himself', and therefore is actively encouraging the practice of private tongue-speaking. I confess that I question whether this is the right deduction to draw. Two reasons make me hesitate.

First, 'edification' in the New Testament is invariably a ministry which builds up others. The Greek word *oikodomeō* means literally 'to build', and is used of building cities, houses, synagogues, *etc.* Used figuratively it is applied to the church. 'I will build my church,' said Jesus (Mt. 16:18). 'You are . . . God's building,' wrote the apostle Paul (1 Cor. 3:9; *cf.* Eph. 2:20, 21), and 'like living stones' are being 'built into a spiritual house', added Peter (1 Pet. 2:5). From this basic meaning the word came to be used of 'strengthening, establishing, edifying' Christians and churches. Luke writes that the Palestinian church was 'being built up', and Paul that his apostolic authority had been given him 'for your upbuilding' (Acts 9:31; 2 Cor. 10:8; 12:19; 13:10). In addition, Christians have a ministry of 'mutual upbuilding' (Rom. 14:19) in which they are to 'build one another up' (1 Thes. 5:11; *cf.* Rom. 15:2; Eph. 4:29; Jude 20). And if it be asked what edifies the church more than anything else, Paul would reply 'truth' (Acts 20:32; *cf.* Col. 2:7) and 'love' (1 Cor. 8:1; *cf.* 10:23). The same emphasis on building up others prevails in 1 Corinthians 14, in that not only does the prophet 'edify' by his message (verses 3, 4) but in public worship 'all things' are to be 'done for edification' (verse 26; cf. verse 17) and all Christians are to 'strive to excel in building up the church' (verse 12; cf. verse 5). Now in the light of this consistent New Testament emphasis on edification as a ministry to others and to the church, what are we to make of the one and only exception, which says that the tongue-speaker 'edifies himself'? Surely there must be at least some degree of irony in what Paul writes, for the phrase is almost a contradiction in terms. Self-edification is simply not what edification is all about in the New Testament.

Secondly, we have to read the expression in the light of the teaching we have already considered that *all* spiritual gifts are service-gifts, bestowed 'for the common good', for ministry to others. How, then, can this one gift be turned in upon itself and be exercised for personal good instead of the common good? Must one not say that this involves a misuse of a gift? What would one think of a believer with a teaching gift who uses it only to give himself private instruction, or of a man with a healing gift who healed no-one but himself? It is hard to justify the self-directed use of a gift specifically bestowed for the benefit of others.

So for these two reasons it seems to me that there must be a note of irony, if not of sarcasm, in Paul's voice as he writes of the tongue-speaker edifying himself. He takes it for granted that the Corinthians, to whom he has clearly explained the purpose of spiritual gifts in chapter 12, will get his meaning and not need him to spell it out any further.

So the *charismata* are all given 'for the common good'. Paul applies this principle in Ephesians 4:11, 12 to the teaching gifts. Christ gifted some to be 'apostles, some prophets, some evangelists, some pastors and teachers'. Why? For what purpose? He goes on: 'to equip the saints for the work of ministry, for building up the body of Christ.' The immediate objective of the teacher is to lead Christian people ('the saints') not only into Christian maturity but also into Christian ministry, to equip them for their ministry in the church and in the world. Pastors are called to be teachers, but this does not mean that they may jealously guard as their own preserve all the ministry of every kind which needs to be done. On the contrary, their ministry is to produce further ministry, as they encourage others to exercise the gifts God has given them. Only then will the further objective be attained, which (again) is the 'building up of the body of Christ' to its full unity and maturity, 'to the measure of the stature of the fullness of Christ' (verses 12, 13).

This glorious goal, which should occupy our minds as it did the apostle Paul's, will be attained through the twin influences of truth and love. It is by 'speaking (or maintaining) the truth in love' that we shall 'grow up in every way into him who is the head, into Christ' (verses 15, 16). Truth is evidently indispensable for the growth into maturity of Christians and churches, for without a full understanding and a strong grasp of God's revealed truth we remain 'children, tossed to and fro and carried about with every wind of doctrine' (verse 14). But truth can be cold and hard if it is not warmed and softened by love. This is why Paul says that ' "knowledge" puffs up, but love builds up' (1 Cor. 8:1). All of us know the pre-eminent influence of love in the healthy emotional development of children. If this is true of the human family, how much more is it true of the family of God? Hence the intrusion of 1 Corinthians 13 between chapters 12 and 14 which are concerned with spiritual gifts. Although the *charismata* are all given for service, for the edification of Christ's body, yet they must be exercised in love if they are to have their intended effect. For without love all gifts, however spectacular, are worthless (13:1–3). So love is the 'still more excellent way', more valuable than even the highest gifts (12:31). Yet there should be no need for us to choose between gifts and love, for in God's purpose they belong together. True love always expresses itself in service, and not least in using the gifts bestowed on us to enable us to serve.

In fact, if love and truth go together, and love and gifts go together, so do love and service, since true love always expresses itself in service. To love is to serve. We are left, then, with these four aspects of Christian life forming a ring or a circle which cannot be broken – love, truth, gifts and service. For love issues in service, service uses the gifts, the highest gift is the teaching of the truth, but truth must be spoken in love. Each involves the others, and wherever you begin all four are brought into operation. Yet 'the greatest of these is love' (13:13).

Conclusion

We began with the 'promise' or 'baptism' of the Spirit, that generous initial gift which God bestows upon us when he takes us to be his own people. Forgiveness and the gift of the Spirit are the obverse and reverse of the comprehensive salvation which is ours in Christ. We should never cease to thank God, with daily wonder, that in his love he first gave his Son to die for us and then gave his Spirit to live in us. Today there is no temple in Jerusalem to which we have to go to meet God; each of us is a temple of God, and so is the local church, for God dwells in us by his Spirit.

Secondly, we need to seek ever more of the Holy Spirit's fullness, by repentance, faith and obedience, and also to keep sowing to the Spirit so that his fruit may grow and ripen in our character. I think I may say with truthfulness that it has been my practice for many years to pray every day that God will fill me with his Spirit and cause more of the Spirit's fruit to appear in my life.

Thirdly, we must always remember that the Holy Spirit is concerned for the church as well as for individual Christians. So we must rejoice equally in his *charis* (grace) given to all, which makes us one, and in his *charismata* (gifts) distributed to all, which make us different. The unity and the diversity of the church are both by his appointment.

We have seen that the gifts are many and varied capacities for service; that at least one is given to every Christian without exception; that they are distributed by the sovereign, gracious will of God, Father, Son and Holy Spirit; and that they are intended 'for the common good', to build up into maturity Christ's body, the church. So let us employ our gifts for one another, 'as good stewards of God's varied grace . . . in order that in everything God may be glorified through Jesus Christ. To him belong glory and dominion for ever and ever. Amen' (I Pet. 4:10, 11).